SERMON OUTLINES ON

THE PSALMS

JOHN PHILLIPS

Exploring Series on Bible Books by John Phillips

Exploring the Old Testament Book by Book
Exploring the New Testament Book by Book

Exploring Psalms (2 volumes)
Exploring Proverbs (2 volumes)
Exploring the Love Song of Solomon
Exploring the Book of Daniel
Exploring the Minor Prophets
Exploring the Gospel of Matthew
Exploring the Gospel of Mark
Exploring the Gospel of Luke
Exploring the Gospel of John
Exploring Acts
Exploring 1 Corinthians
Exploring 2 Corinthians
Exploring Romans
Exploring Galatians
Exploring Ephesians & Philippians
Exploring Colossians & Philemon
Exploring 1 & 2 Thessalonians
Exploring the Pastoral Epistles
Exploring Hebrews
Exploring the Epistle of James
Exploring the Epistles of Peter
Exploring the Epistles of John
Exploring the Epistle of Jude
Exploring Revelation

SERMON OUTLINES ON

THE PSALMS

JOHN PHILLIPS

Kregel
Academic & Professional

Sermon Outlines on the Psalms

© 2012 Betty Jean Phillips

Published by Kregel Publications, a division of Kregel, Inc., P.O.
Box 2607, Grand Rapids, MI 49501

This material was originally published by Loizeaux Brothers,
Neptune, NJ, in *Exploring the Psalms* © 1988 by John Phillips.

ISBN 978-0-8254-4157-8

Printed in the United States of America

12 13 14 15 16 / 5 4 3 2 1

PREFACE

The Psalms are a favorite source of sermon material, and little wonder, for they are rich in human experience! At times they ring with the din and noise of battle; at other times they take us with hushed hearts into the inner sanctuary—into the immediate presence of God. At times they set our hearts aflame and our feet dancing for joy; at other times, when our faces are drenched with tears, we turn to them for comfort. The Psalms are full of the stuff of which life is made and therefore vital to the shepherd's ministry to his flock.

The outlines in this volume, which covers the entire book of Psalms, provide a convenient foundation for the preacher. They have been taken from the author's monumental work, *Exploring the Psalms*, which has been called the best work on the Psalms since *Spurgeon's Treasury of David*. Those in need of illustrative material or a reliable exposition of the text will want to refer to John Phillips's commentary, published in two volumes by this firm.

⁓PSALM 1⁓

THE SAINT AND THE SINNER

I. THE GODLY MAN (1:1–3)
  A. His Path—He Is Separated from the World (1:1)
  He does not:
    1. Listen to the Ungodly Man
    2. Linger with the Sinful Man
    3. Laugh at the Scornful Man
  B. His Pleasure—He Is Satisfied with the Word (1:2)
  God's Word has:
    1. Captured His Full Affection
    2. Claimed His Full Attention
  C. His Prosperity—He Is Situated by the Waters (1:3)
    1. His Prominence
    2. His Permanence
    3. His Position
    4. His Productivity
    5. His Propriety
    6. His Perpetuity
    7. His Prosperity
II. THE GODLESS MAN (1:4–6)
  A. He Is Driven (1:4)
  B. He Is Doomed (1:5)
  C. He Is Damned (1:6)

⮞ PSALM 2 ⮜

REBELS OF THE WORLD, UNITE!

I. GOD'S GUILTY SUBJECTS (2:1–3)
   A. The Formality of Their Rebellion (2:1)
   B. The Force of Their Rebellion (2:2)
   C. The Focus of Their Rebellion (2:3)
II. GOD'S GREAT SCORN (2:4–6)
   A. He Speaks in Derision (2:4)
   B. He Speaks in Displeasure (2:5)
   C. He Speaks in Determination (2:6)
III. GOD'S GLORIOUS SON (2:7–9)
   A. His Sonship (2:7)
   B. His Sovereignty (2:8)
   C. His Severity (2:9)
IV. GOD'S GRACIOUS SPIRIT (2:10–12)

PSALM 3

DAVID AT MAHANAIM

PSALM 4

AN EVENING HYMN

I. SALVATION (4:1–2)
   A. Personal Salvation (4:1)
   B. Practical Salvation (4:2)
II. SANCTIFICATION (4:3–4)
   A. Personal Godliness (4:3)
   B. Personal Goodness (4:4)
III. SACRIFICE (4:5)
   A. The Burnt Offering
   B. The Meal Offering
   C. The Peace Offering
IV. SONG (4:6–7)
   A. The Tragedy of a Joyless Life (4:6)
   B. The Triumph of a Joyful Life (4:7)
V. SECURITY (4:8)

⌒PSALM 5⌒

GOOD MORNING, LORD!

I. DAVID ASKS THE LORD TO LISTEN (5:1–7)
    He wants to talk to Him about:
    A. The Situation (5:1–4)
        1. God Is a Hearing God (5:1–3)
            a. Holy Boldness
            b. Heavy Burdens
            c. Harmonious Beginnings
        2. God Is a Holy God (5:4)
    B. The Sinner (5:5–6)
        1. He Has No Footing (5:5)
        2. He Has No Future (5:6)
    C. The Sanctuary (5:7)
II. DAVID ASKS THE LORD TO LEAD (5:8–9)
III. DAVID ASKS THE LORD TO LEGISLATE (5:10–12)
    A. The Destruction of the Rebel (5:10)
    B. The Delight of the Redeemed (5:11–12)
        1. No Foe Can Daunt Him (5:11)
        2. No Fear Can Haunt Him (5:12)

⌒ PSALM 6 ⌒

A DARK NIGHT

I. DAVID'S SAD CONDITION (6:1–7)
  A. He Speaks About His Excuse: "I am weak" (6:1–5)
    1. His Plight (6:1–3)
      a. Along Spiritual Lines
      b. Along Physical Lines
      c. Along Moral Lines
    2. His Plea (6:4–5)
      a. Along the Line of Mercy
      b. Along the Line of Memory
  B. He Speaks About His Exercise: "I am weary" (6:6–7)
    1. He Was Worn Out (6:6)
    2. He Was Waxing Old (6:7)
II. DAVID'S SUDDEN CONFIDENCE (6:8–10)
  A. His Fears Are Stilled (6:8–9)
  B. His Foes Are Stopped (6:10)

A Loud Cry

I. JUSTIFICATION (7:1–5)
   A. David Trusting (7:1–2)
   B. David Triumphing (7:3–5)
      1. His Positive Assurance
      2. His Positive Assertion
II. JUDGMENT (7:6–16)
   A. David's Desire (7:6–8)
      1. To See God Judge the Sinner (7:6–7)
      2. To See God Judge the Saint (7:8)
   B. David's Defense (7:9–13)
      1. How God's Judgment Works in Principle (7:9–10)
      2. How God's Judgment Works in Practice (7:11–13)
   C. David's Discernment (7:14–16)
      1. Sin in Its Process—Like a Birth (7:14)
      2. Sin in Its Plan—Like a Bait (7:15)
      3. Sin in Its Punishment—Like a Boomerang (7:16)
III. JUBILATION (7:17)

☞ PSALM 8 ☜

DEATH OF A CHAMPION

I. THE LORD'S POSITION (8:1)
II. THE LORD'S POWER (8:2–3)
David saw the Lord as:
   A. Conqueror of the World (8:2)
   B. Creator of the World (8:3)
III. THE LORD'S PRESENCE (8:4–8)
The Mystery of it! That He should:
   A. Come to Us the Way He Does (8:5a)
   B. Care for Us the Way He Does (8:5b–8)
IV. THE LORD'S PORTION (8:9)

⌒PSALM 9⌒

THE FALL OF THE BEAST

I. THE DELIGHT OF THE PROPHET (9:1–2)
    A. Praise the Lord Freely
    B. Praise the Lord Fully
II. THE DESTRUCTION OF THE BEAST (9:3–6)
    A. The Lord's Presence (9:3–4)
        1. We Sense the Thrill with David (9:3)
        2. We See the Throne with David (9:4)
    B. The Lord's Power (9:5–6)
       The destruction of the Beast will be:
        1. Personal (9:5a)
        2. Permanent (9:5b–6a)
        3. Proper (9:6b)
III. THE DAWN OF THE MILLENNIUM (9:7–8)
    A. The Lord's Invincible Majesty (9:7)
    B. The Lord's Inviolate Ministry (9:8)
IV. THE DURATION OF THE TERROR (9:9–14)
    A. The Place of Refuge (9:10)
    B. The Period of Rejoicing (9:11)
    C. The Process of Retribution (9:12–14)
V. THE DAY OF THE LORD (9:15–18)
    A. Something Needing to Be Perceived (9:15–16)
    B. Something Needing to Be Proclaimed (9:17–18)
        1. God's Attitude toward the Nations (9:17)
        2. God's Attitude toward the Needy (9:18)
VI. THE DOCTRINE OF THE PSALM (9:19–20)
    Wicked nations are:
    A. Hindered by God (9:19)
    B. Humbled by God (9:20)

PSALM 10

THE LAWLESS ONE

I. THE LORD IS CONCEALED—WHEN THE
WICKED FLOURISH (10:1–11)
The wicked man's:
A. Seeming Blessing (10:1)
B. Sinful Behavior (10:2)
C. Scornful Boasts (10:3)
D. Stubborn Bias (10:4)
E. Spiritual Blindness (10:5)
F. Swelling Bigotry (10:6)
G. Spoken Blasphemies (10:7)
H. Secret Brutalities (10:8–10)
   1. His Cruelty (the Bandit) (10:8)
   2. His Confidence (the Lion) (10:9a)
   3. His Cunning (the Hunter) (10:9b–ll)
II. THE LORD IS CONCERNED—WHAT THE
WICKED FORGET (19:12–15)
God's eye is on:
A. The Wicked Man's Scornfulness (10:12–13)
B. The Wicked Man's Spitefulness (10:14)
C. The Wicked Man's Sinfulness (10:15)
III. THE LORD IS CROWNED—WHAT THE WICKED FACE (10:16–18)
A. The Lord Will Subdue the Heathen (10:16)
B. The Lord Will Support the Helpless (10:17–18)

15

☞ PSALM 11 ☜

Why Not Run Away and Hide?

I. FEAR IS CONQUERED (11:1–3)
   A. David's Determined Trust (11:1)
   B. David's Developing Troubles (11:2–3)
II. FACTS ARE CONSIDERED (11:4–6)
   A. Where the Lord Sits (11:4a)
   B. What the Lord Sees (11:4b–5)
   C. What the Lord Sends (11:6)
III. FAITH IS CONFESSED (11:7)

PSALM 12

THE DECEITFUL MAN

I. DAVID'S APPEAL (12:1–4)
   A. The Man of God Is Gone from the Earth (12:1)
   B. The Man of Guile Is Great on the Earth (12:2–4)
      1. His Deceitfulness (12:2)
      2. His Downfall (12:3)
      3. His Defiance (12:4)
II. DAVID'S ASSURANCE (12:5–6)
   A. Its Greatness (12:5)
   B. Its Guarantee (12:6)
III. DAVID'S ARMOR (12:7–8)
   A. The Nature of It (12:7)
   B. The Need for It (12:8)

PSALM 13

How Long? How Long? How Long?

I. SORROW (13:1–2)
  A. His Seeming Abandonment (13:1)
   It seemed that God had:
   1. Forgotten Him
   2. Forsaken Him
  B. His Sorrowful Abasement (13:2)
   He has been brought low by:
   1. His Feelings
   2. His Foes
II. SUPPLICATION (13:3–4)
  He tells the Lord he is:
  A. Overwhelmed by His Emotions (13:3)
  B. Overwhelmed by His Enemies (13:4)
III. SONG (13:5–6)
  He is singing because of:
  A. God's Salvation (13:5)
  B. God's Sufficiency (13:6)

THE DEPRAVITY OF MAN

I. THE SUMMONS (14:1–3)
    A. The Case of the Prosecutor (14:1)
       Man is guilty:
       1. In His Innermost Being
       2. In His Iniquitous Behavior
    B. The Calling of the Witness (14:2)
       1. His Person
       2. His Perception
    C. The Conclusion of the Judge (14:3)
       Man stands convicted because of:
       1. His Total Departure
       2. His Total Defilement
       3. His Total Depravity

II. THE SUMMATION (14:4)
    A. Man's Iniquity
    B. Man's Ignorance
    C. Man's Intolerance
    D. Man's Indifference

III. THE SENTENCE (14:5–6)
    A. The Fear It Registered (14:5a)
    B. The Folly It Revealed (14:5b)
    C. The Facts It Rehearsed (14:6)

IV. THE SUSPENSION (14:7)
    A sudden, unexpected:
    A. Note of Hope
    B. Note of Happiness
       is injected into the Psalm

PSALM 15

A Guest in the Lord's House

I. DAVID'S WORSHIP (15:1)
   A. A Pilgrim Worshiper
   B. A Permanent Worshiper
II. DAVID'S WALK (15:2–4)
   A. His Works (15:2a)
   B. His Words (15:2b–4)
      1. His Secret Words (15:2b)
      2. His Spoken Words (15:3–4)
         a. Restrained (15:3a)
         b. Righteous (15:3b)
         c. Respectful (15:4a)
         d. Reliable (15:4b)
III. DAVID'S WAYS (15:5)
   A. They Were Fair (15:5a)
   B. They Were Fixed (15:5b)

PSALM 16

SATISFIED

I. THE PRACTICE OF THE GODLY MAN (16:1–4)
   A. Living in the Lord's Presence (16:1–2)
   B. Living for the Lord's People (16:3)
   C. Living by the Lord's Precepts (16:4)
II. THE PORTION OF THE GODLY MAN (16:5–6)
   A. In the Lord (16:5)
   B. In the Land (16:6)
III. THE PROSPECTS OF THE GODLY MAN (16:7–11)
   A. In This Life (16:7–9)
      1. Guided by God (16:7)
      2. Guarded by God (16:8)
      3. Gladdened by God (16:9)
   B. In That Life (16:10–11)
      1. The Truth of Resurrection (16:10)
      2. The Truth of Rapture (16:11)

⨈ PSALM 17 ⨈

LEST I FORGET GETHSEMANE

I. LORD, HEAR ME! (17:1–6)
   A. I Want You to Examine Me (17:1–2)
   B. I Want You to Exonerate Me (17:3)
   You know:
   1. My Wishes (17:3a)
   2. My Words (17:3b)
   3. My Works (17:4)
   C. I Want You to Exercise Me (17:5–6)
II. LORD, HIDE ME! (17:7–9)
   For You know how to be:
   A. Merciful (17:7a)
   B. Mighty (17:7b)
   C. Moved (17:8–9)
III. LORD, HELP ME! (17:10–15)
   Lord, I am going to:
   A. Tell You about My Circumstances (17:10–12)
   B. Trust You in My Circumstances (17:13–15)
   1. Lord Save Me! (17:13–14)
   2. Lord Satisfy Me! (17:15)

⌐PSALM 18⌐

GREAT DAVID'S GREATER SON

I. THE REJECTED PROPHET (18:1–19)
    A. Trusting at All Times (18:1–3)
    B. Travailing on the Tree (18:4–15)
    We see:
       1. A Tormented Person (18:4–6)
       2. A Tottering Planet (18:7–8)
       3. A Terrible Presence (18:9–11)
       4. A Terrified People (18:12–15)
    C. Triumphing over the Tomb (18:16–19)
II. THE ROYAL PRIEST (18:20–31)
    A. His Authority (18:20–24)
    B. His Activity (18:25–27)
    C. His Ability (18:28–31)
III. THE RETURNING POTENTATE (18:32–50)
    A. Reclaiming the Kingdom for God (18:32–42)
    B. Ruling the Kingdom with God (18:43–48)
    C. Restoring the Kingdom to God (18:49–50)

PSALM 19

THE HEAVENS DECLARE THE GLORY OF GOD

I. GOD'S REVELATION OF HIMSELF
IN THE SKY (19:1–6)
A. An Unmistakable Witness (19:1)
B. An Untiring Witness (19:2)
C. An Understandable Witness (19:3–6)
II. GOD'S REVELATION OF HIMSELF
IN THE SCRIPTURES (19:7–14)
A. God's Word Is Precious (19:7–10)
1. It Challenges Us (19:7)
2. It Cheers Us (19:8)
3. It Changes Us (19:9–10)
B. God's Word Is Powerful (19:11–14)
It has the power to:
1. Convict Us (19:11)
2. Cleanse Us (19:12)
3. Correct Us (19:13–14)
a. It Will Keep Me from Folly (19:13)
b. It Will Keep Me in Fellowship (19:14)

WHEN A NATION GOES TO WAR

I. THE PEOPLE WANT HELP FROM THEIR LEADER (20:1–5)
They want their leader to be one who is:
A. Looking to God (20:1–3)
One who is:
1. Prayerfully in Touch with God (20:1)
2. Powerfully in Touch with God (20:2)
3. Properly in Touch with God (20:3)
B. Listening to God (20:4–5)
So that he might:
1. Plan the Battle Aright (20:4)
2. Pursue the Battle Aright (20:5)
II. THE PRINCE WANTS HELP FROM THE LORD (20:6–9)
A. The Truth He Expressed (20:6)
B. The Trust He Exercised (20:7)
C. The Triumph He Expected (20:8–9)
1. Total Deliverance (20:8)
2. Total Dependence (20:9)

☞ PSALM 21 ☜

Crown Him Lord of All

I. THE SECRET OF THE KING'S STRENGTH—
EXPOSITIONAL (21:1–7)
  A. The Secret Is Disclosed (21:1–2)
    1. The Publication of the Secret (21:1)
    2. The Proof of the Secret (21:2)
  B. The Secret Is Discussed (21:3–7)
    The king's secret strength results in:
    1. Sovereignty (21:3)
    2. Salvation (21:4–6)
    3. Security (21:7)
II. THE SUFFICIENCY OF THE KING'S
STRENGTH—EXPERIENTIAL (21:8–13)
  A. A Kingdom Based on the Power of God (21:8–12)
    1. God's Power to Discover His Foes (21:8)
    2. God's Power to Destroy His Foes (21:9–12)
      a. In a Passionate Way (21:9)
      b. In a Permanent Way (21:10)
      c. In a Purposeful Way (21:11–12)
  B. A Kingdom Based on the Preeminence of God (1:13)

PSALM 22

DARK CALVARY

I. THE TERRIBLE REALITY OF CALVARY (22:1–21)
A. Abandoned by God (22:1–6)
The gulf between Christ and:
1. The Holiness of God (22:1–3)
2. The Holiest of Men (22:4–6)
B. Abhorred by Men (22:7–18)
1. The Contempt of Men (22:7–10)
2. The Cruelty of Men (22:11–17)
3. The Callousness of Men (22:18)
C. Abused by Satan (22:19–21)
II. THE TREMENDOUS RESULTS OF CALVARY (22:22–31)
A. The Lord as Priest (22:22–26)
In view of:
1. His Resurrection (22:22)
2. His Return (22:23–26)
a. The Nation of Israel (22:23–24)
b. The Church of God (22:25)
c. The Nations of Mankind (22:26)
B. The Lord as Prince (22:27–31)
1. He Is Acclaimed as King (22:27–29)
a. Converting the Nations (22:27)
b. Controlling the Nations (22:28)
c. Contenting the Nations (22:29)
2. He Is Proclaimed as King (22:30–31)

PSALM 23

THE SHEPHERD PSALM

I. THE SECRET OF A HAPPY LIFE (23:1–3)
    It has:
    A. Its Roots in a Magnificent Spiritual Relationship
    B. Its Results in a Magnificent Spiritual Reality
       The Good Shepherd:
       1. Shares His Life with Us
       2. Gives His Life for Us
       3. Puts His Life in Us

II. THE SECRET OF A HAPPY DEATH (23:4–5)
    David talks about
    A. The Tomb
       We have the assurance of:
       1. The Lord's Presence
       2. The Lord's Protection
    B. The Table

III. THE SECRET OF A HAPPY ETERNITY (23:6)

THE KING COMES HOME

I.   THE LORD'S CLAIM (24:1–2)
II. THE LORD'S CALL (24:3–6)
    A. The Question Asked (24:3–4)
    B. The Question Answered (24:5–6)
III. THE LORD'S COMING (24:7–10)
    A. The First Challenge (24:7–8)
    B. The Further Challenge (24:9–10)

PSALM 25

GUIDE ME, OH THOU GREAT JEHOVAH

I. DAVID'S PLEA (25:1–14)
   A. David's Concern as a Believer (25:1–7)
      1. Lord, Protect Me (25:1–3)
      2. Lord, Pilot Me (25:4–5)
         a. He Was Wanting to Be Led (25:4)
         b. He Was Willing to Be Led (25:5a)
         c. He Was Waiting to Be Led (25:5b)
      3. Lord, Pardon Me (25:6–7)
   B. David's Confidence as a Believer (25:8–14)
      1. The Priorities of Guidance (25:8–9)
         a. A Person Must Be Saved (25:8)
         b. A Person Must Be Submissive (25:9)
      2. The Principles of Guidance (25:10–11)
         a. Consecration (25:10)
         b. Confession (25:11)
      3. The Prerequisites of Guidance (25:12–14)
         a. A Right Attitude Toward the Lord (25:12–13)
         b. A Right Attitude Toward the Word (25:14)
II. DAVID'S PLIGHT (25:15–22)
   A. How He Proceeded to Evaluate His Plight (25:15–19)
      1. His Difficulty (25:15)
      2. His Desolation (25:16)
      3. His Distress (25:17)
      4. His Disgrace (25:18)
      5. His Danger (25:19)
   B. How He Planned to Evade His Plight (25:20–22)
      1. As a Person (25:20–21)
      2. As a Prince (25:22)

PSALM 26

Search Me, Oh God

I. A DIVINELY OPEN LIFE (26:1–2)
II. A DIVINELY OBEDIENT LIFE (26:3)
III. A DIVINELY OVERCOMING LIFE (26:4–6)
   A. The Principle of Separation (26:4–5)
   B. The Principle of Sanctification (26:6)
IV. A DIVINELY OVERFLOWING LIFE (26:7–8)
   Overflowing in the direction of:
   A. Praising the Lord (26:7a)
   B. Preaching the Lord (26:7b)
   C. Pursuing the Lord (26:8)
V. A DIVINELY OBSTRUCTED LIFE (26:9–10)
VI. A DIVINELY ORDERED LIFE (26:11–12)

A MERCURIAL TEMPERAMENT

I. TRUSTING ON THE HIGHLANDS OF FAITH (27:1–6)
A. David's Intelligent Delight in the Lord (27:1–3)
Based on:
1. The Lord's Personal Dealings (27:1)
2. The Lord's Past Dealings (27:2)
3. The Lord's Promised Dealings (27:3)
B. David's Intense Desire for the Lord (27:4–6)
1. Wanting to Enjoy the Presence of the Lord in His House (27:4)
a. A Deliberate Passion
b. A Daily Passion
c. A Discerning Passion
2. Wanting to Enjoy the Protection of the Lord in His House (27:5–6)
He wanted the Lord to:
a. Hide Him (27:5)
b. Help Him (27:6)

II. TREMBLING ON THE LOWLANDS OF FEAR (27:7–14)
David wanted a fresh experience of:
A. The Grace of God (27:7–10)
   Note:
   1. How Repentant He Was (27:7–8)
   2. How Rejected He Was (27:9–10)
   Rejected, so he felt, by:
      a. His Father in Heaven (27:9)
      b. His Family on Earth (27:10)
B. The Guidance of God (27:11–12)
   He needed:
   1. Direction (27:11)
   2. Deliverance (27:12)
C. The Goodness of God (27:13–14)
   1. What Saved Him—The Trust Element in Focus (27:13)
   2. What Strengthened Him—The Time Element in Focus (27:14)

———•———

PSALM 28

THE LORD'S MY ROCK

I. THE REQUEST (28:1–5)
  A. David's Invocation (28:1–2)
    He invokes:
    1. The Word of God (28:1)
    2. The Word with God (28:2)
  B. David's Invitation (28:3–5)
    He invites the Lord to:
    1. Deliver Him (28:3)
      a. No Rest
      b. No Rules
      c. No Restraint
    2. Destroy them (28:4–5)
      a. Righteously (28:4)
      b. Reasonably (28:5)
II. THE RESULT (28:6–9)
  A. A Note of Praise (for himself) (28:6–7)
    1. He Has Been Heard (28:6)
    2. He Has Been Helped (28:7)
  B. A Note of Prayer (for others) (28:8–9)
    That they might know:
    1. The Strength of God (28:8)
    2. The Salvation of God (28:9a)
    3. The Satisfaction of God (28:9b)

HE RIDES UPON THE STORM

I. THE LORD'S PREEMINENCE (29:1–2)

II. THE LORD'S POWER (29:3–9)

    A. Over the Sea—The Lord's Dealing with the Natural Man (29:3–4)

    B. Over Lebanon—The Lord's Dealings with the Spiritual Man (29:5–6)

    C. Over the Wilderness—The Lord's Dealings with the Carnal Man (29:7–9)

III. THE LORD'S PEOPLE (29:10–11)

    A. Owning His Sovereignty (29:10)

    B. Owning His Sufficiency (29:11)

PSALM 30

JOY COMETH IN THE MORNING

I. DAVID'S PROTECTION (30:1–3)
   A. From Scornful Men (30:1)
   B. From Serious Maladies (30:2–3)
II. DAVID'S PRAISE (30:4–5)
   A. For God's Character (30:4)
   B. For God's Compassion (30:5)
III. DAVID'S PRESUMPTION (30:6–7)
   A. His Spiritual Pride Remembered (30:6–7)
      1. What He Had Felt (30:6–7a)
      2. What He Had Forgotten (30:7b)
   B. His Spiritual Pride Rebuked (30:7b)
IV. DAVID'S PRAYER (30:8–10)
   A. His Approach (30:8)
   B. His Appeal (30:9)
   C. His Application (30:10)
V. DAVID'S PROCLAMATION (30:11–12)
   A. How Greatly His Life Had Been Changed (30:11)
      1. The Inward Proof
      2. The Outward Proof
   B. How Gloriously His Life Had Been Channeled (30:12)

LIFE'S UPS AND DOWNS

I. SALVATION AND STRENGTH (31:1–4)
   A. David's Desire (31:1)
   B. David's Defense (31:2–3)
   C. David's Danger (31:4)
II. SURRENDER AND SONG (31:5–8)
   A. The Redeemed Man (31:5)
   B. The Righteous Man (31:6)
   C. The Rejoicing Man (31:7–8)
      1. God Is Merciful (31:7a)
      2. God Is Mindful (31:7b)
      3. God Is Masterful (31:8)
III. SORROW AND SHAME (31:9–13)
   A. The Completeness of David's Grief (31:9–10)
      1. Encompassing Grief (31:9)
      2. Endless Grief (31:10a)
      3. Exhaustless Grief (31:10b)
   B. The Cause of David's Grief (31:11–13)
      1. He Was Forsaken (31:11)
      2. He Was Forgotten (31:12)
      3. He Was Fearful (31:13)

IV. SUPPLICATION AND SCORN (31:14–18)
   A. The Prayer for Victory (31:14–16)
   B. The Prayer for Vengeance (31:17–18)
V. SAFETY AND SYMPATHY (31:19–22)
   A. The Goodness of God (31:19)
   B. The Greatness of God (31:20)
   C. The Graciousness of God (31:21–22)
      1. How Wonderful He Is (31:21)
      2. How Wicked I Am (31:22)
VI. SWEETNESS AND STABILITY (31:23–24)
   A. Love for the Lord Urged (31:23)
   B. Loyalty to the Lord Urged (31:24)

———•———

PSALM 32

THE SIN QUESTION

I. SIN AS SEEN BY THE SINNER (32:1–7)
    A. The Pleasure We Feel When Sin Is Cleansed (32:1–2)
        1. Sin Is a Defiance (32:1a)
        2. Sin Is a Defect (32:1b)
        3. Sin Is a Distortion (32:2a)
        4. Sin Is a Deception (32:2b)
    B. The Penalty We Face When Sin Is Concealed (32:3–4)
        David had once been:
        1. A Healthy Man (32:3)
        2. A Happy Man (32:4a)
        3. A Hearty Man (32:4b)
    C. The Pardon We Find When Sin Is Confessed (32:5)
    D. The Path We Follow When Sin Is Conquered (32:6–7)
        1. The Power of Prayer (32:6a)
        2. The Power of Position (32:6b–7a)
        3. The Power of Peace (32:7b)
        4. The Power of Praise (32:7c)
II. SIN AS SEEN BY THE SAVIOUR (32:8–11)
    We need to be:
    A. Guided (32:8)
    B. Governed (32:9)
    C. Guarded (32:10)
    D. Gladdened (32:11)

PSALM 33

FROM EVERLASTING THOU ART GOD

I. THE LORD AND HIS PRAISE (33:1–3)
We are to praise Him:
A. Thankfully (33:1)
B. Thoroughly (33:2)
C. Thoughtfully (33:3)
II. THE LORD AND HIS POWER (33:4–9)
A. The Moral Power of His Word (33:4–5)
B. The Manifest Power of His Word (33:6–7)
C. The Moving Power of His Word (33:8)
D. The Matchless Power of His Word (33:9)
III. THE LORD AND HIS PROVIDENCE (33:10–19)
A. The Nations and Their Decisions (33:10–12)
1. Those That Rebel at God's Word (33:10–11)
2. Those That Respond to God's Word (33:12)
B. The Nations and Their Destinies (33:13–19)
The Lord looks at:
1. Their Communities (33:13–14)
2. Their Characteristics (33:15)
3. Their Conflicts (33:16–17)
4. Their Calamities (33:18–19)
IV. THE LORD AND HIS PEOPLE (33:20–22)
A. The Help of the Saved (33:20)
B. The Happiness of the Saved (33:21)
C. The Hope of the Saved (33:22)

PSALM 34

THE GOLIATHS OF GATH

I. DAVID'S PRAISE (34:1–10)
  A. What He Resolved (34:1–3)
  B. What He Remembered (34:4–6)
    1. His Danger—"I was lost" (34:4)
    2. His Discernment—"I looked" (34:5)
    3. His Deliverance—"I was liberated" (34:6)
  C. What He Realized (34:7–10)
    1. God Protects (34:7)
    2. God Provides (34:8–10)
II. DAVID'S PROCLAMATION (34:11–22)
  A. The Summons (34:11)
  B. The Subject (34:12)
  C. The Sermon (34:13–20)
    1. Listen to My Exposition (34:13–16)
      a. Watch Your Words (34:13)
      b. Watch Your Walk (34:14)
      c. Watch Your Works (34:15)
    2. Learn from My Example (34:17–20)
  D. The Summary (34:21–22)

PSALM 35

WHEN FRIENDS BECOME FOES

I. IN THE CAMP—DAVID AS A WARRIOR (35:1–10)
    A. What He Wants for His Foes (35:1–8)
       He wants them to be:
       1. Defeated (35:1–3)
       2. Destroyed (35:4–8)
    B. What He Wants for His Fears (35:9–10)
       He wants them dissolved by:
       1. The Joy of the Lord (35:9)
       2. The Justice of the Lord (35:10)
II. IN THE COURT—DAVID AS A WITNESS (35:11–17)
    A. David's Plight (35:11–12)
    B. David's Plea (35:13–17)
III. IN THE CLOISTER—DAVID AS A WORSHIPER (35:18–28)
    A. A Praising Man (35:18)
    B. A Praying Man (35:19–27)
       1. Informing the Lord (35:19–21)
       2. Invoking the Lord (35:22–27)
    C. A Proclaiming Man (35:28)

PSALM 36

A STUDY IN CONTRASTS

I. THE SINFUL MAN (36:1–4)
   A. The Sinful Man's Persuasion (36:1)
   B. The Sinful Man's Pride (36:2)
   C. The Sinful Man's Policy (36:3a)
   D. The Sinful Man's Past (36:3b)
   E. The Sinful Man's Plans (36:4a)
   F. The Sinful Man's Path (36:4b)
II. THE SAVED MAN (36:5–12)
   Rests in the loving kindness of God, which is backed by:
   A. The Righteousness of God's Throne (36:5–6)
      1. It Cannot Be Matched (36:5)
      2. It Cannot Be Moved (36:6a)
      3. It Cannot Be Measured (36:6b)
   B. The Resources of God's Throne (36:7–9)
      We can be:
      1. Wonderfully Sure (36:7)
      2. Wonderfully Satisfied (36:8)
      3. Wonderfully Saved (36:9)
   C. The Responsibilities of God's Throne (36:10–12)
      1. To Justify the Saint (36:10–11)
         a. Permanently (36:10)
         b. Practically(36:11)
      2. To Judge the Sinner (36:12)

PSALM 37

WHEN WICKEDNESS TRIUMPHS ON EARTH

I. PROSPECTS THAT ARE FOREIGN TO
   THE WICKED (37:1–11)
   The righteous man's:
   A. Discovery (37:1–2)
   B. Dwelling (37:3)
   C. Delight (37:4)
   D. Dependence (37:5–6)
   E. Discipline (37:7)
   F. Deliverance (37:8–10)
   G. Domains (37:11)

II. PURSUITS THAT ARE FAVORED BY
    THE WICKED (37:12–22)
    The wicked man's:
    A. Plots (37:12–13)
    B. Power (37:14–15)
    C. Prosperity (37:16–17)
    D. Protection (37:18–20)
    E. Pledge (37:21–22)

III. PATHS THAT ARE FORSAKEN BY
     THE WICKED (37:23–31)
     The righteous man's:
     A. Walk (37:23–24)
     B. Wants (37:25)
     C. Works (37:26–27)
     D. Welfare (37:28–29)
     E. Wisdom (37:30–31)

IV. POINTS THAT ARE FORGOTTEN BY
   THE WICKED (37:32–40)
   He forgets that:
   A. Truth Is on the Side of the Godly (37:32–34)
   B. Time Is on the Side of the Godly (37:35–36)
   C. Trust Is on the Side of the Godly (37:37–40)
      1. A Perfect Standing (37:37–38)
      2. A Perfect Stability (37:39–40)

PSALM 38

SICKNESS AND SUFFERING
BROUGHT ON BY SIN

I. DAVID'S SIN (38:1–4)
    A. The Consequences of It (38:1–3)
        1. Divine Anger (38:1–2)
        2. Daily Anguish (38:3)
    B. The Consciousness of It (38:4)
II. DAVID'S SUFFERING (38:5–8)
    A. Disgusted (38:5)
    B. Distressed (38:6)
    C. Diseased (38:7)
    D. Disturbed (38:8)
III. DAVID'S SORROW (38:9–14)
    His sorrows were:
    A. Spiritual (38:9–10)
    B. Social (38:11–12)
    C. Silent (38:13–14)
IV. DAVID'S SUPPLICATION (38:15–22)
    A. Lord, Hear Me (38:15–16)
    B. Lord, Heal Me (38:17–18)
    C. Lord, Help Me (38:19–22)
        1. Consider What My Situation Is (38:19–20)
        2. Consider Who My Savior Is (38:21–22)

PSALM 39

ALTOGETHER VANITY

I. DAVID'S PLEDGE (39:1–3)
   A. The Importance of It (39:1)
   B. The Impropriety of It (39:2)
   C. The Impossibility of It (39:3)
II. DAVID'S PLEA (39:4–5)
   He wanted the answer to:
   A. Life's Frailty (39:4)
   B. Life's Futility (39:5)
III. DAVID'S PLIGHT (39:6–11)
   It was the plight of:
   A. The Wealthy Man (39:6)
   B. The Wicked Man (39:7–11)
      He must therefore face:
      1. The Reality of His Sin (39:7–9)
         a. He Needed a Savior (39:7–8)
         b. He Needed a Spokesman (39:9)
      2. The Results of His Sin (39:10–11)
         a. He Had Lost His Blessedness (39:10)
         b. He Had Lost His Beauty (39:11a)
         c. He Had Lost His Bearings (39:11b)
IV. DAVID'S PLAN (39:12–13)
   To ask God to make him:
   A. Happy Again (39:12a)
   B. Holy Again (39:12b)
   C. Healthy Again (39:13)

PSALM 40

PAST TRIUMPHS AND PRESENT TROUBLES

I. DAVID'S CONVICTION (40:1–5)
   A. The Reason for It (40:1–3a)
      1. He Heard Me (40:1)
      2. He Helped Me (40:2–3a)
   B. The Result of It (40:3b–5)
      He became:
      1. A Soul Winner (40:3b–4)
      2. A Spiritual Worshiper (40:5)
II. DAVID'S CONSECRATION (40:6–8)
   A. Truth Realized in His Life (40:6–7)
      1. The Truth Concerning Ritual (40:6)
      2. The Truth Concerning Reality (40:7)
   B. Truth Reproduced in His Life (40:8)
III. DAVID'S CONFESSION (40:9–10)
   A. The Righteous Majesty of God (40:9–10a)
   B. The Rich Mercy of God (40:10b)
IV. DAVID'S CONTRITION (40:11–13)
   David sees:
   A. The Lord and His Suffering (40:11–12c)
   B. The Lord and Our Sins (40:12b)
   C. The Lord and God's Strength (40:13)
V. DAVID'S CONSOLATION (40:14–17)
   A. God Is Mighty (40:14)
   B. God Is Magnified (40:15–16)
   C. God Is Merciful (40:17)

⁓ PSALM 41 ⁓

THE CONSPIRACY

I. DAVID'S FEARS (41:1–3)
A. His Condition Is Described (41:1)
B. His Confidence Is Described (41:2)
C. His Consolation Is Described (41:3)
II. DAVID'S FOES (41:4–9)
A. They Professed Concern for Him (41:4–6)
   He contemplates:
   1. The Horror of His Sin (41:4)
   2. The Hatred of His Subjects (41:5)
   3. The Hypocrisy of His Son (41:6)
B. They Promoted Conspiracy Against Him (41:7–9)
   1. The Strength of This Conspiracy (41:7–8)
      a. His Past Wickedness (41:7)
      b. His Present Weakness (41:8)
   2. The Sting of This Conspiracy (41:9)
III. DAVID'S FAITH (41:10–13)
   He has:
   A. A Merciful God (41:10)
   B. A Mighty God (41:11)
   C. A Marvelous God (41:12–13)

⟨PSALM 42⟩

THE THIRSTY SOUL

I. HEZEKIAH'S DISAPPOINTMENT (42:1–5)
   A. His Spiritual Barrenness (42:1–2)
   B. His Spiritual Bitterness (42:3–4)
   C. His Spiritual Boldness (42:5)
II. HEZEKIAH'S DESPAIR (42:6–8)
   A. He Was Overwhelmed (42:6–7)
   B. He Was Overjoyed (42:8)
III. HEZEKIAH'S DECISION (42:9–11)
   A. Henceforth He Would Talk to the Lord (42:9–10)
      1. Lord! Remember Your Own Nature (42:9)
      2. Lord! Remember Your Own Name (42:10)
   B. Henceforth He Would Trust in the Lord (42:11)

PSALM 43

RUMBLINGS IN THE NORTH

I. THE ADVERSARY HE FOUGHT (43:1–2)
   A. Hezekiah's Desire (43:1a)
   B. Hezekiah's Danger (43:1b)
   C. Hezekiah's Discernment (43:2a)
   D. Hezekiah's Doubt (43:2b)
II. THE ADVANCE HE SOUGHT (43:3–4)
   A. In His Personal Motivation (43:3)
      1. To Apprehend the Truth
      2. To Appropriate the Truth
   B. In His Public Ministry (43:4)
      1. To Lead the People in Sacrifice
      2. To Lead the People in Song
III. THE ADVICE HE BOUGHT (43:5)
   Let me examine the reason:
   A. Why I Am Sad
   B. Why I Am Safe
   C. Why I Am Sure

PSALM 44

HOW TO PRAY FOR ONE'S COUNTRY

I. ISRAEL'S PREVIOUS HISTORY (44:1–8)
   A. The Facts of That History (44:1–3)
   B. The Force of That History (44:4–8)
II. ISRAEL'S PRESENT HELPLESSNESS (44:9–22)
   A. The Military Disaster Confronting the Nation (44:9–16)
      They were being:
      1. Defeated (44:9–10)
      2. Deported (44:11–12)
      3. Derided (44:13–16)
   B. The Moral Dilemma Confronting the Nation (44:17–22)
      1. The Religious Revival It Had Experienced (44:17–19)
      2. The Remarkable Resolve It Had Expressed (44:20–21)
         a. Challenging God on All Counts (44:20–21)
         b. Choosing God at All Costs (44:22)
III. ISRAEL'S POSITIVE HOPE (44:23–26)
   A call upon God to:
   A. Regard His People (44:23–25)
   B. Rescue His People (44:26)

⌒PSALM 45⌒

HIS ROYAL MAJESTY ... HER ROYAL MAJESTY

I. HIS ROYAL MAJESTY (45:1–8)
   A. His Majesty's Grace (45:1–2)
      1. The Bliss of the Lord's People (45:1)
      2. The Beauty of the Lord's Person (45:2)
   B. His Majesty's Glory (45:3–5)
      He is glorious in:
      1. His Magnificence (45:3)
      2. His Ministry (45:4a)
      3. His Might (45:4b–5)
   C. His Majesty's Government (45:6–8)
      It is:
      1. A Permanent Government (45:6)
      2. A Perfect Government (45:7a)
      3. A Pleasant Government (45:7b)
      4. A Prosperous Government (45:8)

II. HER ROYAL MAJESTY (45:9–17)
  A. Her Majesty's Coming (45:9)
  B. Her Majesty's Calling (45:10–11)
    She is to:
    1. Want Her Lord (45:10)
    2. Win Her Lord (45:11a)
    3. Worship Her Lord (45:11b)
  C. Her Majesty's Court (45:12)
    1. Her Presence Is Acknowledged
    2. Her Power Is Acknowledged
  D. Her Majesty's Character (45:13–14a)
  E. Her Majesty's Companions (45:14b–15)
  F. Her Majesty's Career (45:16)
  G. Her Majesty's Crown (45:17)

—•—

PSALM 46

A MIGHTY FORTRESS IS OUR GOD

I. THE REFUGE (46:1–3)
  A. How Personal It Is (46:1a)
  B. How Powerful It Is (46:1b)
  C. How Permanent It Is (46:2–3)
II. THE RIVER (46:4–7)
  A. How Impassive Is Its Flow (46:4)
  B. How Impotent Is Its Foe (46:5–7)
    Note:
    1. The Marvelous River (46:4)
    2. The Mysterious Resident (46:5–7)
III. THE RULER (46:8–11)
  A. The Call to Behold (46:8–9)
  B. The Call to Believe (46:10–11)
    1. In God's Person (46:10a)
    2. In God's Plan (46:10b)
    3. In God's Presence (46:11)

PSALM 47

A MILLENNIAL HYMN

I. THE GREAT PREDICTION (47:1–4)
A. The Basis of the Prediction (47:1–2)
1. The Voice of Triumph It Employs (47:1)
2. The Vision of Truth It Embodies (47:2)
B. The Breadth of the Prediction (47:3–4)
1. Israel's Ultimate Power (47:3)
2. Israel's Unique Privilege (47:4)
II. THE GREAT PROCLAMATION (47:5–9)
A. We Must Sing His Praise (47:5–7)
1. The Rapture of Christ to Glory (47:5)
2. The Reception of Christ in Glory (47:6)
3. The Return of Christ from Glory (47:7)
B. We May See His Power (47:8–9)
1. The Throne Is Seen (47:8)
2. The Throng Is Seen (47:9)
a. The Gathering of the People (47:9a)
b. The Guarantee of the Peace (47:9b)

⁀PSALM 48⁀

WHEN THE DRUMS OF WAR ARE STILLED

I. THE IMPOSSIBLE TASK (48:1–8)
   A. The Difficult Terrain That Warned the Foe (48:1–2)
   The mountain of:
     1. God's Abiding Presence (48:1)
     2. God's Absolute Power (48:2)
   B. The Disturbing Truth That Worried the Foe (48:3)
   C. The Deadly Terror That Weakened the Foe (48:4–6)
   How the enemy:
     1. Found the City (48:4)
     2. Fled the City (48:5)
     3. Feared the City (48:6)
   D. The Disastrous Troubles That Wasted the Foe (48:7–8)
II. THE IMPERISHABLE TRUTH (48:9–14)
   A. The Kind of Love That God Imparts (48:9–10)
     1. It Promotes Worship (48:9)
     2. It Promotes Witness (48:10)
   B. The Kind of Liberty That God Imparts (48:11–13)
     1. It Lets out the Feelings (48:11)
     2. It Leans on the Facts (48:12)
     3. It Looks to the Future (48:13)
   C. The Kind of Life That God Imparts (48:14)
     1. Deathless
     2. Directed

PSALM 49

WORTHLESS WEALTH

I. THE SUBJECT OF RICHES FORMALLY INTRODUCED (49:6)
  A. The Poet Is Introduced (49:1–4)
    1. His Proclamation (49:1–2)
    2. His Promise (49:3–4)
  B. The Problem Is Introduced (49:5–6)
    1. The Wickedness That Dogs a Man's Heels (49:5)
    2. The Wealth That Devours a Man's Hopes (49:6)
II. THE SUBJECT OF RICHES FULLY INVESTIGATED (49:7–20)
  A. Worldly Wealth Produces Spiritual Blindness (49:7–12)
    1. The Rich Man Confuses Truth with Error (49:7–9)
      a. What He Cannot Purchase (49:7)
      b. What He Cannot Perceive (49:8)
      c. What He Cannot Prevent (49:9)
    2. The Rich Man Confuses Time with Eternity (49:10–12)
      a. What He Sees (49:10)
      b. What He Says (49:11)
      c. What He Shows (49:12)
  B. Worldly Wealth Promotes Spiritual Banality (49:13)
  C. Worldly Wealth Provokes Spiritual Bankruptcy (49:14–20)
    The rich fool is:
    1. Robbed of His Future (49:14–15)
    2. Robbed of His Fortune (49:16–18)
    3. Robbed of His Faith (49:19–20)

PSALM 50

THE JUDGMENT OF ISRAEL

I. THE JUDGMENT OF ISRAEL IS IMPENDING (50:1–6)
A. The Sudden Announcement (50:1)
B. The Solemn Appearing (50:2–3)
C. The Sobered Assembly (50:4–6)
  1. The Jury Is Present (50:4)
  2. The Jew Is Present (50:5)
  3. The Judge Is Present (50:6)
II. THE JUDGMENT OF ISRAEL IS IMPERATIVE (50:7–23)
A. The Weighing of the Proof (50:7–21)
  1. Dead Works Judged (50:7–15)
    a. The Peerless Name of the Accuser (50:7)
    b. The Punishable Nature of the Accusation (50:8–12)
    c. The Proven Need of the Accused (50:13–15)
  2. Downright Wickedness Judged (50:16–21)
    a. The Worst Kind of Blasphemy (50:16–17)
    b. The Worst Kind of Behavior (50:18)
    c. The Worst Kind of Betrayal (50:19–20)
    d. The Worst Kind of Belief (50:21)
B. The Warning of the People (50:22–23)
  1. The Suspended Sentence (50:22)
  2. The Promised Pardon (50:23)

PSALM 51

The Sword of Nathan

I. DAVID'S CONFESSION (51:1–6)
  A. Lord, Be Merciful in My Need (51:1–4a)
    1. I Am Very Sinful (51:1–2)
    2. I Am Very Sorry (51:3–4a)
      I cannot escape:
      a. The Ghost That Haunts Me (51:3)
      b. The Guilt That Horrifies Me (51:4a)
  B. Lord, Be Mindful of My Nature (51:4b–6)
    1. I Was Born in Sin (51:4b–5)
    2. I Am Blinded by Sin (51:6)
II. DAVID'S CLEANSING (51:7–12)
  He wanted the Lord to deal with:
  A. Sin's Defilement (51:7)
  B. Sin's Deafness (51:8)
  C. Sin's Disgrace (51:9)
  D. Sin's Damage (51:10)
  E. Sin's Doom (51:11)
  F. Sin's Depression (51:12a)
  G. Sin's Defeat (51:12b)
III. DAVID'S CONSECRATION (51:13–19)
  A. The Life He Would Not Forsake (51:13–15)
    1. He Would Continue to Preach (51:13)
    2. He Would Continue to Pray (51:14–15)
  B. The Lessons He Would Never Forget (51:16–19)
    1. The Personal Truth He Had Learned (51:16–17)
    2. The Prophetic Truth He Had Learned (51:18–19)

PSALM 52

DOEG, THE EDOMITE

I. THE WICKEDNESS OF DOEG (52:1–5)
  A. What Doeg Did (52:1–4)
    1. Doeg's Paraded Triumph (52:1)
    2. Doeg's Poisoned Tongue (52:2)
    3. Doeg's Perverted Temperament (52:3–4)
  B. What Doeg Deserved (52:5)
II. THE WELL-BEING OF DAVID (52:6–9)
  A. The Strengthening of David's Friends (52:6–7)
  B. The Strengthening of David's Faith (52:8–9)

PSALM 53

THE DOWNFALL OF ISRAEL'S FOES

I. A WICKED WORLD (53:1–4)
   A. The Foolish Man (53:1)
      1. His False Concepts
      2. His Foul Conduct
      3. His Faulty Character
   B. The Forgetful Man (53:2)
   C. The Filthy Man (53:3)
   D. The Fierce Man (53:4)
II. A WARRING WORLD (53:5)
   A. The Dread Which Overtakes the Foe
   B. The Defeat Which Overtakes the Foe
   C. The Disgrace Which Overtakes the Foe
III. A WONDERFUL WORLD (53:6)
   A. Salvation
   B. Security
   C. Song

⌒PSALM 54⌒

BETRAYED

I. DAVID'S FIRST REACTION TO THE TREACHERY (54:1–3)
   A Threefold Plea Based on:
   A. God's Name (54:1)
   B. David's Need (54:2)
   C. His Foes' Nature (54:3)
      1. So Foreign to Him
      2. So Friendless to Him
      3. So Foolish to Him
II. DAVID'S FURTHER REACTION TO
    THE TREACHERY (54:4–5)
    A. "I Have a Reliable God" (54:4)
    B. "I Have a Righteous God" (54:5)
III. DAVID'S FINAL REACTION TO THE TREACHERY (54:6–7)
    A. His Promise (54:6)
       1. To Sacrifice (54:6a)
       2. To Sing (54:6b)
    B. His Premise (54:7)

PSALM 55

WHEN SORROWS LIKE SEA BILLOWS ROLL

I. DAVID'S ANGUISH (55:1–8)
  A. What David Felt (55:1–3)
    1. Abandoned by God (55:1–2)
    2. Abused by Men (55:3)
  B. What David Feared (55:4–5)
  C. What David Fancied (55:6–8)
II. DAVID'S ANGER (55:9–15)
  A. At the Trouble in His Country (55:9–11)
    1. A Possible Solution (55:9)
    2. A Present Situation (55:10–11)
  B. At the Treachery of His Comrade (55:12–15)
III. DAVID'S ANSWER (55:16–23)
  A. The Response of God (55:16–18)
    1. David Will Pray Boldly (55:16–17)
    2. David Will Pray Believingly (55:18)
  B. The Righteousness of God (55:19–21)
    1. Past History Demonstrates That God Would Act (55:19a)
    2. Present Happenings Demand That God Should Act (55:19b–21)
      a. David's foes were:
      b. Disbelieving Men (55:19b)
      c. Despicable Men (55:20)
      d. Deceitful Men (55:21)
  C. The Retribution of God (55:22–23)
      a. God's Defense of the Saint (55:22)
      b. God's Defeat of the Sinner (55:23)

PSALM 56

WHEN FEAR MEETS FAITH

I. GOD IS MERCIFUL (56:1–4)
    A. David's Foes (56:1–2)
       1. Their Perpetual Animosity (56:1)
       2. Their Personal Animosity (56:2)
    B. David's Faith (56:3–4)
       1. When He Would Exercise It (56:3)
       2. Why He Would Exercise It (56:4)

II. GOD IS MINDFUL (56:5–11)
    A. Of David's Trials (56:5–7)
       1. The Pressure of His Enemies—Sore! (56:5–6)
       2. The Punishment of His Enemies—Sure! (56:7)
    B. Of David's Tears (56:8–9)
    C. Of David's Trust (56:10–11)

III. GOD IS MIGHTY (56:12–13)
     The thought made David:
     A. Happy in His Soul (56:12–13a)
     B. Heedful of His Steps (56:13b)

⌐PSALM 57⌐

HIDE ME, OH MY SAVIOR, HIDE

I. THE CALAMITIES WHICH THRONGED HIM (57:1–3)
   A. Lord, Hide Me (57:1)
   B. Lord, Hear Me (57:2)
   C. Lord, Help Me (57:3)
      By saving me from:
      1. Injury
      2. Injustice
II. THE CRISIS WHICH THREATENED HIM (57:4–6)
   A. The Seriousness of His Situation (57:4)
   B. The Sovereignty of His Savior (57:5)
   C. The Significance of His Salvation (57:6)
III. THE CONFIDENCE WHICH THRILLED HIM (57:7–11)
   A. A Willing Confidence (57:7)
   B. A Witnessing Confidence (57:8–9)
      1. Enthusiastic: Witnessing to the Very Creation (57:8)
      2. Evangelistic: Witnessing to the Various Countries (57:9)
         a. The Nation of Israel
         b. The Neighbors of Israel
   C. A Worshiping Confidence (57:10–11)
      1. God's Mercy Was Its Theme (57:10)
      2. God's Majesty Was Its Theme (57:11)

⌒PSALM 58⌒

THE DISHONEST JUDGE

I. JUSTICE VIOLATED (58:1–5)
  A. The Unjust Judge Examined (58:1)
  B. The Unjust Judge Exposed (58:2–5)
    1. The Source of His Wickedness (58:2a)
    2. The Scope of His Wickedness (58:2b–3)
      a. Ingrown in the Nation (58:2b)
      b. Ingrained in Their Natures (58:3)
    3. The Stubbornness of His Wickedness (58:4–5)
II. JUSTICE VISUALIZED (58:6–9)
  The fate of the unjust judge is likened to:
  A. A Disarmed Lion (58:6)
  B. A Drying Stream (58:7a)
  C. A Destroyed Weapon (58:7b)
  D. A Dissolving Snail (58:8a)
  E. A Discontinued Pregnancy (58:8b)
  F. A Disrupted Meal (58:9)
III. JUSTICE VINDICATED (58:10–11)
  A. Irrepressible Praise (58:10)
  B. Irrefutable Proof (58:11)

PSALM 59

BEWARE OF THE DOGS

I. DAVID'S DANGER (59:1–9)
   A. His Plea (59:1–2)
   B. His Panic (59:3–5)
      1. What Concerned Him (59:3)
      2. What Controlled Him (59:4)
      3. What Consoled Him (59:5)
   C. His Peril (59:6–9)
      1. How He Viewed the Peril of His Situation (59:6–7)
      2. How He Vanquished the Peril to His Soul (59:8–9)
II. DAVID'S DELIVERANCE (59:10–17)
   A. His Protection (59:10–15)
      1. His Confidence (59:10)
      2. His Conviction (59:11–15)
      He wanted:
   B. His People to Be Able to Recognize God's Judgment (59:11–12)
   C. His Persecutors to Be Able to Recognize God's Justice (59:13–15)
   D. His Praise (59:16–17)

⌒PSALM 60⌒

WHEN KINGS GO FORTH TO WAR

I. DAVID'S CONSTERNATION (60:1–5)
  A. A National Defeat (60:1–3)
    1. A Spiritual Disaster (60:1)
    2. A Strategic Disaster (60:2)
    3. A Sobering Disaster (60:3)
  B. A Notable Deliverance (60:4–5)
    1. God's Banner Is Seen (60:4)
    2. God's Beloved Is Saved (60:5)
II. DAVID'S CONQUEST (60:6–9)
  A. How David Quelled His Fears (60:6–8)
    1. Reasserting the Sovereignty of the Nation of Israel
       (60:6–7)
    2. Reaffirming the Subjection of the Neighbors of Israel
       (60:8)
  B. How David Questioned His Future (60:9)
III. DAVID'S CONCERN (60:10–11)
  A. The Painful Truth to Realize About Israel's Weakness
     (60:10)
  B. The Practical Truth to Remember About Israel's
     Weakness (60:11)
IV. DAVID'S CONFIDENCE (60:12)

PSALM 61

MIXED FEELINGS

I. THE EXILED KING (61:1–4)
   A. David's Request (61:1–2)
     1. Lord, Hear Me (61:1)
     2. Lord, Help Me (61:2a)
     3. Lord, Hide Me (61:2b)
   B. David's Reason (61:3)
   C. David's Resolve (61:4)
II. THE EXPECTANT KING (61:5–8)
   A. Rejoicing in God's Kindness (61:5)
   B. Resting in God's Kindness (61:6–7)
   David wanted God to:
     1. Marvelously Prolong His Life (61:6)
     2. Mercifully Preserve His Life (61:7)
   C. Responding to God's Kindness (61:8)

BE STILL, MY SOUL

I. DAVID'S ADVERSARY—HE ADDRESSES
   HIMSELF TO HIS SITUATION (62:1–4)
   A. Where His Defense Lies (62:1–2)
      1. His Salvation Is in God (62:1–2a)
      2. His Security Is in God (62:2b)
   B. Where His Danger Lies (62:3–4)
      1. His Enemies Were Pushing Against Him (62:3)
      2. His Enemies Were Plotting Against Him (62:4)

II. DAVID'S ADVICE—HE ADDRESSES
    HIMSELF TO HIS SOUL (62:5–7)
    A. Be Still (62:5)
    B. Be Sure (62:6)
    C. Be Strong (62:7)

III. DAVID'S ADMONITION—HE ADDRESSES
     HIMSELF TO HIS SUBJECTS (62:8–12)
     A. The Question of Trust (62:8–10)
        1. Trusting Aright (62:8)
           a. When We Should Trust the Lord
           b. Why We Should Trust the Lord
        2. Trusting Amiss (62:9–10)
           a. Trusting in Men (62:9)
           b. Trusting in Might (62:10a)
           c. Trusting in Money (62:10b)
     B. The Question of Truth (62:11–12)
        1. The Word of God (62:11)
        2. The Ways of God (62:12)
           a. It Is a Merciful Way (62:12a)
           b. It Is a Moral Way (62:12b)

PSALM 63

KNOCKED DOWN BUT NOT KNOCKED OUT

I. HOW DAVID LONGED FOR GOD (63:1–3)
    A. Where He Was (63:1)
    B. What He Wanted (63:2)
    C. Why He Worshiped (63:3)
II. HOW DAVID LIVED FOR GOD (63:4–8)
    A. He Worked for God (63:4)
    B. He Witnessed to God (63:5)
    C. He Waited for God (63:6–7)
    D. He Walked with God (63:8)
III. HOW DAVID LOOKED FOR GOD (63:9–11)
    A. He Looked for Victory (63:9–10)
       1. His Foes Doomed (63:9)
       2. His Foes Defeated (63:10a)
       3. His Foes Devoured (63:10b)
    B. He Looked for Vindication (63:11)

The Poisonous Tongue

I. DAVID'S DETRACTORS (64:1–6)
    A. David Feared Their Malice (64:1–2)
       He was very much aware of:
       1. His Danger (64:1)
       2. Their Dislike (64:2)
    B. David Feared Their Methods (64:3–6)
       He tells the Lord:
       1. How They Sharpened up Their Tongues (64:3a)
       2. How They Shot at Their Target (64:3b–4)
       3. How They Shared in Their Treachery (64:5–6)
          a. Their Common Bond (64:5)
          b. Their Criminal Bent (64:6)
II. DAVID'S DEFENDER (64:7–10)
    A. God Would Reward the Sinner (64:7–8)
    B. God Would Remind the Spectator (64:9)
    C. God Would Rejoice the Saint (64:10)

PSALM 65

HALLELUJAH FOR THE HARVEST

I. APPROACHING GOD (65:1–4)
    A. A Silent People (65:1)
    B. A Seeking People (65:2)
    C. A Sinful People (65:3)
    D. A Satisfied People (65:4)
II. APPREHENDING GOD (65:5–8)
    A. God's Power to Convert (65:5)
       1. The Hebrew People (65:5a)
       2. The Heathen Peoples (65:5b)
    B. God's Power to Create (65:6)
    C. God's Power to Control (65:7–8)
       1. The Restless Waves (65:7a)
       2. The Restless World (65:7b–8)
III. APPRECIATING GOD (65:9–13)
    A. The Prodigality of the Heavens (65:9–10)
    B. The Prodigality of the Harvests (65:11–13)

PSALM 66

MORE ABOUT THE MILLENNIUM

I. THE HAPPY MAN (66:1–4)
   A. The Vision Poetical (66:1–2)
   B. The Vision Prophetical (66:3–4)
      1. God's Irresistible Might (66:3)
      2. God's Irrevocable Millennium (66:4)
II. THE HUMBLED MAN (66:5–12)
   A. Humbled by the Mighty Works of God (66:5–7)
      1. An Invitation (66:5)
      2. An Illustration (66:6)
      3. An Implication (66:7)
   B. Humbled by the Marvelous Ways of God (66:8–12)
      1. In Protecting Israel (66:8–9)
      2. In Proving Israel (66:10–12a)
      3. In Prospering Israel (66:12b)
III. THE HOLY MAN (66:13–20)
   A. His Trustworthiness (66:13–15)
      1. His Resolve (66:13)
      2. His Recollection (66:14)
      3. His Reckoning (66:15)
   B. His Testimony (66:16–20)
      1. What He Declared (66:16)
      2. What He Did (66:17)
      3. What He Discovered (66:18–20)
         a. Guilt Hinders Prayer (66:18)
         b. God Hears Prayer (66:19)
         c. Grace Helps Prayer (66:20)

☞ PSALM 67 ☜

A CAMEO OF THE MILLENNIUM

I. THE DAWNING SUNRISE OF THE MILLENNIUM—
   THE HOPE OF IT! (67:1–3)
   A. The Need for the Millennium (67:1)
      1. How Dreadful (67:1a)
      2. How Dismal (67:1b)
      3. How Dark (67:1c)
   B. The Nature of the Millennium (67:2–3)
      1. Undiluted Wisdom (67:2a)
      2. Unlimited Welfare (67:2b)
      3. Unfailing Worship (67:3)
II. THE DAYTIME SPLENDOR OF THE MILLENNIUM—
   THE HEIGHT OF IT! (67:4–6)
   A. Moral Blessing for the Nations (67:4–5)
      1. Spontaneous Joy (67:4a)
      2. Splendid Justice (67:4b)
      3. Spiritual Jubilation (67:5)
   B. Material Blessing for the Nations (67:6)
III. THE DISTANT SHADOW OF THE
   MILLENNIUM—THE HINT OF IT! (67:7)
   A. The Fullness at the End of the Era
   B. The Fear at the End of the Earth

⌒PSALM 68⌒

MARCHING TO ZION

I. ISRAEL'S BRILLIANT PAST (68:1–18)
   A. Her Sovereign Helper (68:1–6)
      1. God's Might (68:1–3)
      2. God's Majesty (68:4)
      3. God's Mercy (68:5–6)
      4. God's Morality (68:6c)
   B. Her Significant History (68:7–10)
   C. Her Spiritual Heritage (68:11–14)
   D. Her Splendid Homeland (68:15–18)
      1. The High Places of Israel (68:15–16)
      2. The Holy Places of Israel (68:17–18)
II. ISRAEL'S BLESSED PROSPECTS (68:19–35)
   A. Israel Preserved Among the Nations (68:19–23)
      1. The Exile Endured (68:19–20)
      2. The Exile Ended (68:21–23)
   B. Israel Promoted Above the Nations (68:24–35)
      1. Where Power Will Reside (68:24–27)
      2. Why Peace Will Reign (68:28–31)
         a. Worship Will Be Absolute (68:28–29)
         b. Warfare Will Be Abolished (68:30–31)
      3. When Praise Will Ring (68:32–35)

⁐PSALM 69⁐

THE FLOODTIDES OF WRATH

I. THE VOICE OF ONE CRYING IN THE
WILDERNESS (69:1–21)
A. His Desperate Plight (69:1–12)
1. His Woes (69:1–6)
a. He Displays His Feelings (69:1–3)
(1) His Fears (69:1–2)
(a) Sin Was Destroying Him (69:1)
(b) Sin Was Defiling Him (69:2a)
(c) Sin Was Drowning Him (69:2b)
(2) His Tears (69:3)
b. He Describes His Foes (69:4)
c. He Discloses His Fate (69:5)
d. He Declares His Faith (69:6)
2. His Ways (69:7–12)
a. He Is Reproached (69:7)
b. He Is Rejected (69:8)
c. He Is Righteous (69:9–11)
(1) His Consuming Devotion Godward (69:9)
(2) His Continuing Denial Selfward (69:10)
(3) His Convicting Distress Manward (69:11)
d. He Is Ridiculed (69:12)
B. His Desperate Plea (69:13–21)
1. "Hear Me" (69:13–17)
a. God's Mercies Are Multiplied (69:13–15)
(1) He Declares His Confidence (69:13)
(2) He Describes His Condition (69:14–15)
b. God's Mercies Are Magnified (69:16–17)
(1) Wonderfully Defined (69:16)
(2) Willingly Displayed (69:17)

2. "Help Me" (69:18–21)
   a. Lord, Move Near to Me (69:18)
   b. Lord, Make Note of Me (69:19–21)
      (1) The Scorn I Am Facing (69:19)
      (2) The Sorrow I Am Facing (69:20)
         (a) I Am in No Condition to Bear It (69:20a)
         (b) I Have No Companion to Share It (69:20b)
      (3) The Suffering I Am Facing (69:21)
II. THE VOICE OF ONE CURSING IN THE
WILDERNESS (69:22–28)
   A. The Curse Expressed (69:22–25)
   He wanted his enemies':
      1. Homes to Be Cursed (69:22)
      2. Health to Be Cursed (69:23)
      3. Happiness to Be Cursed (69:24)
      4. Houses to Be Cursed (69:25)
   B. The Curse Explained (69:26)
   C. The Curse Expanded (69:27–28)
   He wanted his enemies to have:
      1. No Hope of Salvation on Earth (69:27)
      2. No Hope of Salvation in Eternity (69:28)
III. THE VOICE OF ONE CALLING IN THE
WILDERNESS (69:29–36)
   A. His Condition (69:29)
   B. His Confidence (69:30–31)
      1. Praising the Lord (69:30)
      2. Pleasing the Lord (69:31)
   C. His Conviction (69:32–34)
      1. His Testimony Will Be Heeded (69:32)
      2. His Trust Will Be Honored (69:33)
      3. His Triumph Will Be Heralded (69:34)
   D. His Contention (69:35–36)
      1. About the Cities of Judah (69:35)
      2. About the Citizens of Judah (69:36)

⌒ PSALM 70 ⌒

LORD, MAKE HASTE!

I. A CALL (70:1)
II. A CONTRAST (70:2–4)
   A. David's Foes (70:2–3)
      1. What They Sought (70:2)
      2. What They Said (70:3)
   B. David's Friends (70:4)
III. A CONFESSION (70:5)
   A. Lord, I Am a Poor Man (70:5a)
   B. Lord, I Am a Praying Man (70:5b)

PSALM 71

A Godly Old Man

I. THE TRIALS OF A GODLY OLD MAN (71:1–6)
  A. His Expression of God's Faithfulness (71:1–3)
    1. He States His Case (71:1–2)
    2. He States His Confidence (71:3)
  B. His Experience of God's Faithfulness (71:4–6)
    1. Where He Goes in His Trial (71:4)
    2. What He Knows in His Trial (71:5–6a)
    3. Why He Grows in His Trial (71:6b)
II. THE TROUBLES OF A GODLY OLD MAN (71:7–13)
  A. The Problem He Was Finding (71:7)
  B. The Praise He Was Formulating (71:8)
  C. The Pressure He Was Feeling (71:9)
  D. The Persecution He Was Facing (71:10–11)
  E. The Prayer He Was Focusing (71:12–13)
III. THE TRUST OF A GODLY OLD MAN (71:14–16)
  A. This Old Man's Song (71:14–15)
    1. A Growing Song (71:14)
    2. A Great Song (71:15)
  B. This Old Man's Strength (71:16)
IV. THE TESTIMONY OF A GODLY OLD MAN (71:17–24)
  A. To the Past (71:17)
  B. To the Present (71:18–19)
    1. A Passionate Appeal to God (71:18)
    2. A Personal Appreciation of God (71:19)

C. To the Prospect (71:20–24)
   1. A Glorious Resurrection by God (71:20)
   2. A Glorious Reign with God (71:21)
   3. A Glorious Response to God (71:22–24)
      a. His Life Will Be Full of Melody (71:22–23)
      b. His Lips Will Be Full of Messages (71:24)

☞ PSALM 72 ☜

A SONG OF SOLOMON

I. THE COMING KING (72:1–4)
   A. His Gifts (72:1)
   B. His Grace (72:2)
   C. His Glory (72:3–4)
II. THE COMING KINGDOM (72:5–20)
   A. Irreversible in Its Permanence (72:5–7)
      1. Established by Divine Compulsion (72:5)
      2. Established in Divine Compassion (72:6)
      3. Established with Divine Cooperation (72:7)
   B. Irresistible in Its Power (72:8–11)
      1. The Extent of That Power (72:8)
      2. The Exercise of That Power (72:9)
      3. The Examples of That Power (72:10)
      4. The Exuberance of That Power (72:11)
   C. Irreproachable in Its Principles (72:12–15)
      1. The Welfare of Mankind (72:12–14)
      2. The Wealth of Mankind (72:15a)
      3. The Worship of Mankind (72:15b)
   D. Irrefutable in Its Prosperity (72:16–17)
      1. The Outlook for That Day (72:16)
      2. The Outcome in That Day (72:17)
   E. Irrepressible in Its Praise (72:18–20)
      1. A Full Doxology (72:18–19)
      2. A Final Declaration (72:20)

PSALM 73

THE DECEITFULNESS OF RICHES

I. THE PROBLEM STATED (73:1–3)
   A. The Psalmist's Confidence (73:1)
   B. The Psalmist's Confession (73:2–3)
      1. The Serious Consequences of His Doubt (73:2)
      2. The Significant Cause of His Doubt (73:3)
II. THE PROBLEM STUDIED (73:4–16)
   A. Computing Its Complexity (73:4–9)
      1. The Seeming Blessings of the Ungodly (73:4–5)
      2. The Sinful Behavior of the Ungodly (73:6)
      3. The Solid Benefits of the Ungodly (73:7)
      4. The Soaring Blasphemies of the Ungodly (73:8–9)
   B. Compounding Its Perplexity (73:10–16)
      1. What the Wicked Said (73:10–11)
      2. What the Writer Said (73:12–16)
      He confessed:
         a. The Pernicious Private Consequences of Thinking Like the Wicked (73:12–14)
         b. The Potential Public Consequences of Thinking Like the Wicked (73:15)
         c. The Painful Personal Consequences of Thinking Like the Wicked (73:16)

III. THE PROBLEM SOLVED (73:17–28)
  A. The Psalmist's Own Foolishness (73:17–22)
    1. How Could I Be So Blind? (73:17–20)
      a. Where He Stood when His Eyes Were Opened (73:17)
      b. What He Said when His Eyes Were Opened (73:18–19)
    2. How Could I Be So Dumb? (73:20–22)
  B. The Psalmist's Own Future (73:23–26)
    His future is now filled with the vision of:
    1. God's Presence (73:23)
    2. God's Protection (73:24)
    3. God's Person (73:25)
    4. God's Provision (73:26)
  C. The Psalmist's Own Faith (73:27–28)
    1. The Consequences of a Godless Life (73:27)
    2. The Confidence of a Godly Life (73:28)

$\backsim$PSALM 74$\backsim$

THE ENEMY IN THE SANCTUARY

I. THE DIMENSIONS OF THE TROUBLE (74:1–3)
A. Lord, Why Have You Abandoned Your Own People? (74:1)
B. Lord, Why Have You Abandoned Your Own Possessions? (74:2a–b)
C. Lord, Why Have You Abandoned Your Own Place? (74:2c–3)

II. THE DESECRATION OF THE TEMPLE (74:4–9)
A. The Congregation (74:4)
B. The Contrast (74:5–6)
C. The Conflagration (74:7)
D. The Conspiracy (74:8)
E. The Confusion (74:9)

III. THE DARKNESS OF THE TIMES (74:10–11)
A. God's Seeming Delay (74:10)
B. God's Seeming Distance (74:11)

IV. THE DEFENSE OF THE TRUTH (74:12–17)
A. National Phenomena (74:12)
B. Natural Phenomena (74:13–17)

V. THE DISGRACE OF THE TESTIMONY (74:18–23)
A. Lord, Remember Your People (74:18–19)
B. Lord, Respect Your Promise (74:20)
C. Lord, Rekindle Your Praise (74:21)
D. Lord, Reveal Your Power (74:22–23)

⌒ PSALM 75 ⌒

THE CUP OF GOD'S WRATH

I. GOD IS SOVEREIGN IN HIS PERSON (75:1)
II. GOD IS SOVEREIGN IN HIS POWER (75:2–3)
  A. He Judges Righteously (75:2–3a)
  B. He Judges Rightfully (75:3b)
III. GOD IS SOVEREIGN IN HIS PURPOSES (75:4–7)
  A. The Question of Human Pride (75:4–5)
  B. The Question of Human Promotion (75:6–7)
IV. GOD IS SOVEREIGN IN HIS PUNISHMENTS (75:8)
  A. The Depths of the Cup
  B. The Drinking of the Cup
  C. The Dregs of the Cup
V. GOD IS SOVEREIGN IN HIS PRAISE (75:9–10)
  A. The Joy He Bestows (75:9)
  B. The Justice He Bestows (75:10)

⌒ PSALM 76 ⌒

WHEN GOD STEPS IN

I. WE HAVE A FAMOUS GOD (76:1–6)
   A. Where His Fame Was Known (76:1–2)
      1. The Country Named (76:1)
      2. The Capital Named (76:2)
   B. Why His Fame Was Known (76:3–6)
      1. The Mighty Defeat of the Foe (76:3–4)
         a. Its Greatness (76:3)
         b. Its Glory (76:4)
      2. The Miraculous Defeat of the Foe (76:5–6)
II. WE HAVE A FEARFUL GOD (76:7–12)
   A. He Is to Be Recognized for What He Is (76:7–9)
      1. The Irresistible Power of God (76:7)
      2. The Irrefutable Proof of God (76:8–9)
   B. He Is to Be Revered for Who He Is (76:10–12)
      1. Sinners Must Revere Him (76:10)
      2. Saints Must Revere Him (76:11)
      3. Sovereigns Must Revere Him (76:12)

PSALM 77

When All Around Is Dark

I. SIGHING (77:1–9)
  A. The Psalmist Prays (77:1–3)
    1. Deliberately (77:1)
    2. Despairingly (77:2)
    3. Desperately (77:3)
  B. The Psalmist Ponders (77:4–6)
    1. Why He Pondered (77:4)
    2. What He Pondered (77:5–6)
      a. The Past Exploits of God (77:5)
      b. His Personal Experience of God (77:6)
  C. The Psalmist Probes (77:7–9)
    1. The Permanence of the Situation (77:7–8)
    2. The Perplexities of the Situation (77:9)
II. SINGING (77:10–20)
  A. What the Psalmist Resolved (77:10–12)
    1. To Revive His Memory (77:10–11)
    2. To Redirect His Meditations (77:12)
  B. What the Psalmist Realized (77:13–15)
    1. The Secret (77:13a)
    2. The Solution (77:13b–15)
  C. What the Psalmist Recalled (77:16–20)
    1. How God Liberated in the Past (77:16–19)
    2. How God Led in the Past (77:20)

⌒PSALM 78⌒

THE VOICE OF HISTORY

I. THE PSALMIST DECLARES HIS THEME (78:1–11)
   A. An Explanation (78:1–3)
   B. An Exhortation (78:4–11)
      1. If You Do Indoctrinate Your Children (78:4–7)
      2. If You Don't Indoctrinate Your Children (78:8–11)
II. THE PSALMIST DEVELOPS HIS THEME (78:12–72)
   A. The Period of Divine Rule (78:12–66)
      1. The Triumphant Period of Israel's Salvation (78:12–16)
         a. How God Delivered Israel (78:12)
         b. How God Directed Israel (78:13–16)
      2. The Tragic Period of Israel's Sins (78:17–66)
         a. The Lust of the Flesh (78:17–39)
         b. The Lure of the World (78:40–55)
         c. The Lies of the Devil (78:56–66)
   B. The Period of Davidic Rule (78:67–72)
      1. The People God Chose: Judah, Not Joseph (78:67–68a)
      2. The Place God Chose: Zion, Not Shiloh (78:68b–69)
      3. The Person God Chose: David, Not Saul (78:70–72)

☞PSALM 79☜

Help! Help!

I. THE PRAYER (79:1–12)
   A. Why the Psalmist Prayed (79:1–4)
      1. The Desecration of the Sanctuary (79:1)
      2. The Decimation of the Saints (79:2–3)
      3. The Defamation of the Scornful (79:4)
   B. What the Psalmist Prayed (79:5–12)
      1. For the Lord to Hurry (79:5)
      2. For the Lord to Heed (79:6–8)
         a. The Wickedness of the Heathen (79:6–7)
         b. The Weakness of the Hebrews (79:8)
      3. For the Lord to Help (79:9–12)
         An appeal to:
         a. The Lord's Name (79:9)
         b. The Lord's Nearness (79:10)
         c. The Lord's Nature (79:11–12)
II. THE PROMISE (79:13)

PSALM 80

THE RAVAGED VINEYARD

I. THE VENGEANCE OF GOD (80:1–7)
   A. The Lord Does Not Assure Our Protection Anymore (80:1–3)
      1. Lord, Shadows Are About Us (80:1–2)
      2. Lord, Shine Out upon Us (80:3)
   B. The Lord Does Not Answer Our Prayers Anymore (80:4–7)
      1. Lord, Heed Our Plight (80:4–6)
      2. Lord, Hear Our Plea (80:7)
II. THE VINEYARD OF GOD (80:8–19)
   A. The Royal Vine (80:8–11)
      1. The Planet Was Sovereignly Procured (80:8)
      2. The Place Was Specially Prepared (80:9a)
      3. The Plan Was Sufficiently Prosperous (80:9b–11)
   B. The Ruined Vine (80:12–13)
      1. The Fences Have Been Destroyed (80:12)
      2. The Fruit Has Been Devoured (80:13)
   C. The Restored Vine (80:14–19)
      1. The Prayer for Restoration (80:14–16)
      2. The Process of Restoration (80:17–19)
         a. A Man from God (80:17)
         b. A Miracle by God (80:18)
         c. A Movement of God (80:19)

PSALM 81

OPPORTUNITIES LOST FOREVER

I. THE FEAST OF THE LORD (81:1–5)
   A. The Psalmist Is Aroused in Jubilation (81:1–4)
      1. He Is a Happy Man (81:1–3)
         a. The Occupation That Involved Him (81:1–2)
         b. The Occasion That Inspired Him (81:3)
      2. He Is a Holy Man (81:4)
   B. The Psalmist Is Arrested by Jehovah (81:5)

II. THE FEATS OF THE LORD (81:6–7)
   A. Whence He Took Them (81:6)
   B. What He Taught Them (81:7a)
   C. Where He Tried Them (81:7b)

III. THE FEAR OF THE LORD (81:8–16)
   A. How Israel Received the Commandments (81:8–10)
      1. The Lord's Call (81:8)
      2. The Lord's Claim (81:9)
      3. The Lord's Compassion (81:10)
   B. How Israel Rejected the Commandments (81:11–16)
      1. Their Consuming Lust (81:11–12)
      2. Their Continuing Loss (81:13–16)
      They lost out because:
         a. Morally, the Lord Left Them to Their Folly (81:13)
         b. Militarily, the Lord Left Them to Their Foes (81:14–15)
         c. Materially, the Lord Left Them to Their Famines (81:16)

PSALM 82

THE JUDGES ARE JUDGED

I. THE SUPREME COURT (82:1)
   A. The Lord's Position
   B. The Lord's Purpose

II. THE SERIOUS COMPLAINT (82:2)
   A. The Continual Injustice of the Judges
   B. The Criminal Injustice of the Judges

III. THE STRINGENT COMMAND (82:3–4)
   A. To Defend the Poor (82:3)
   B. To Deliver the Poor (82:4)

IV. THE SWIFT CONVICTION (82:5)
   A. The Reason for Their Corruption
   B. The Result of Their Corruption

V. THE SOLEMN CONDEMNATION (82:6–7)
   A. Their High Office Is Extolled (82:6)
   B. Their Hideous Offense Is Exposed (82:7)

VI. THE SECOND COMING (82:8)
   A. The Lord Will Return
   B. The Lord Will Reign

⌐PSALM 83⌐

THE TEN-NATION CONFEDERACY

I. THE VICIOUS FOES OF ISRAEL (83:1–8)
   A. The United Purpose of the Foe (83:1–5)
      1. Their Pagan Character (83:1–2)
      2. Their Prior Conference (83:3)
      3. Their Prime Concern (83:4)
      4. Their Popular Cause (83:5)
   B. The United Power of the Foe (83:6–8)
      1. Nations More or Less Related to Israel (83:6–7)
      2. Nations More or Less Remote from Israel (83:8)
II. THE VANQUISHED FOES OF ISRAEL (83:9–18)
   A. God Rules over All Nations (83:9–12)
      1. How God Delivered Israel by Physical Means—
         A Sudden Tempest Overthrew the Canaanites
         in the Days of Barak (83:9–10)
      2. How God Delivered Israel by Psychological Means—
         A Secret Terror Overwhelmed the Midianites
         in the Days of Gideon (83:11–12)
   B. God Rules over All Nature (83:13–18)
      1. The Psalmist Seeks God's Power (83:13–15)
      2. The Psalmist Sees God's Purpose (83:16–17)
      3. The Psalmist Sings God's Praise (83:18)

PSALM 84

LORD, I'M COMING HOME

I. DWELLING IN THE SANCTUARY OF GOD (84:1–4)
   A. Our Love (84:1)
   B. Our Longings (84:2)
   C. Our Looks (84:3)
      1. The Sparrow
      2. The Swallow
      3. The Sovereign
   D. Our Life (84:4)
II. DRAWING ON THE STRENGTH OF GOD (84:5–8)
   A. Our Heart Is Right (84:5)
   B. Our Highway Is Rough (84:6–7)
      1. Weeping in the Valley (84:6)
      2. Walking on the Mountain (84:7)
   C. Our Hope Is Real (84:8)
III. DELIGHTING IN THE SERVICE OF GOD (84:9–12)
   A. We Are Here, Lord (84:9)
      1. We Resign All Our Worries
      2. We Realize All Our Wants
   B. We Are Home, Lord (84:10)
      1. Time Takes on a New Dimension
      2. Tasks Take on a New Distinction
   C. We Have Been Helped, Lord (84:11)
   D. We Are Happy, Lord (84:12)

PSALM 85

A PRAYER FOR REVIVAL

I. THE REQUEST (85:1–7)
  A. Praise for God's Forgiveness (85:1–3)
    1. The Favor of God (85:1)
    2. The Forgiveness of God (85:2)
    3. The Fury of God (85:3)
  B. Prayer for God's Fullness (85:4–7)
    1. National Repentance Is Needed (85:4–5)
    2. National Revival Is Needed (85:6–7)
II. THE REPLY (85:8–13)
  A. The Neglect of God's Salvation (85:8)
  B. The Nearness of God's Salvation (85:9)
  C. The Nature of God's Salvation (85:10–13)
    1. Its Mighty Principles (85:10–11)
    2. Its Material Prosperity (85:12)
    3. Its Moral Progress (85:13)

PSALM 86

THE MERCY SEAT

I. HIS PLEADING CRY (86:1–4)
A. What He Was (86:1–2a)
1. His Humility (86:1)
2. His Holiness (86:2a)
B. What He Wanted (86:2b–4)
II. HIS PEERLESS CONCEPTS (86:5–10)
A. A Merciful God (86:5–7)
B. A Mighty God (86:8–10)
1. Looking at the Past: A World Formed as the Work of God (86:8)
2. Looking at the Prospect: A World Founded on the Worship of God (86:9)
3. Looking at the Present: A World Filled with the Wonders of God (86:10)
III. HIS PRIMARY CONCERN (86:11–13)
A. To Be a Teachable Person (86:11)
B. To Be a Triumphant Person (86:12–13)
IV. HIS PERSONAL CONDITION (86:14)
V. HIS POWERFUL CONVICTIONS (86:15–17)
A. A Compassionate God (86:15)
B. A Capable God (86:16)
C. A Considerate God (86:17)

⌐PSALM 87⌐

JERUSALEM! JERUSALEM!

I. THE PRIMARY APPEAL OF THIS PSALM
    A. The Royal City (87:1–3)
        1. Its Foundations (87:1)
        2. Its Favor (87:2)
        3. Its Fame (87:3)
    B. The Roll Call (87:4)
        1. Egypt—Chosen for Its Resplendent Past
        2. Babylon—Chosen for Its Religious Power
        3. Philistia—Chosen for Its Racial Pride
        4. Tyre—Chosen for Its Renowned Prosperity
        5. Ethiopia—Chosen for Its Remote Position
    C. The Regal Claim (87:5–6)
        1. A Splendid Certainty (87:5)
        2. A Special Citation (87:6)
    D. The Ringing Climax (87:7)
II. THE PROPHETIC APPROACH TO THIS PSALM
III. THE PERSONAL APPLICATION OF THIS PSALM

PSALM 88

THE LEPER'S CRY

I. NO FUTURE LEFT (88:1–7)
   A. His Despondent Cry (88:1)
   B. His Despairing Cry (88:2)
   C. His Desperate Cry (88:3–7)
      1. His Present Weakness (88:3–4)
      2. His Personal Wretchedness (88:5–6)
      3. His Past Wrongfulness (88:7)

II. NO FRIENDS LEFT (88:8)

III. NO FOUNDATION LEFT (88:9–12)
   A. His Hopeless Attitude (88:9)
   B. His Hopeless Appeal (88:10–12)
   How can the dead respond to:
      1. God's Mighty Power (88:10)
      2. God's Marvelous Pity (88:11)
      3. God's Moral Purity (88:12)

IV. NO FAITH LEFT (88:13–18)
   A. He Is Forsaken (88:13–14)
      1. No Expectation in His Prayers (88:13)
      2. No Explanation for His Plight (88:14)
   B. He Is Fearful (88:15–17)
   C. He Is Friendless (88:18)

$\backsim$ PSALM 89 $\backsim$

THE DAVIDIC COVENANT

I. THE ACTUAL SIGNIFICANCE OF THE COVENANT (89:1–4)
A. The Principles Involved (89:1–2)
B. The Person Involved (89:3)
C. The Promise Involved (89:4)
II. THE ABSOLUTE SECURITY OF THE COVENANT (89:5–18)
A. God's Power in Heaven (89:5–8)
1. The Heavenly Court (89:5–6)
2. The Heavenly Chorus (89:7–8)
B. God's Power in History (89:9–18)
1. The Revelation of That Power (89:9–13)
a. Revealed in Conquest (89:9–10)
b. Revealed in Creation (89:11–13)
2. The Response to That Power (89:14–18)
He praises God for:
a. His Righteous Principles (89:14)
b. His Redeemed People (89:15–16)
c. His Royal Protection (89:17–18)
III. THE AMAZING SPLENDOR OF THE COVENANT (89:19–37)
A. Made with David Personally (89:19–28)
1. It Was Majestic in Expression (89:12–23)
a. The Divine Initiative (89:19–20)
b. The Divine Incentive (89:21–23)

—·—

PSALM 90

LIFE AT ITS BEST IS VERY BRIEF

I. THE RIGHT PERSPECTIVE (90:1–6)
  A. The Sovereignty of God (90:1–2)
    1. He Is a Tremendous God (90:1)
    2. He Is a Tender God (90:1)
    3. He Is a Timeless God (90:2)
  B. The Sympathy of God (90:3–4)
    1. He Knows the Tyranny the Tomb Has over Us (90:3)
    2. He Knows the Tyranny That Time Has over Us (90:4)
  C. The Severity of God (90:5–6)
II. THE REAL PROBLEM (90:7–12)
  A. Our Lives Are So Sinful (90:7–8)
  B. Our Lives Are So Short (90:9–10)
  C. Our Lives Are So Serious (90:11–12)
III. THE RESULTING PRAYER (90:13–17)
  A. A Fresh Evidence of the Moving of God (90:13)
  B. A Fresh Enduement of the Mercy of God (90:14–15)
  C. A Fresh Expression of the Might of God (90:16)
  D. A Fresh Effulgence of the Majesty of God (90:17)

PSALM 91

THE HIDING PLACE

I. IN TIMES OF TRIAL (91:1–4)
   A. His Fortress (91:1–2)
      1. Elyon, "The Most High": Possession (91:1)
      2. Shaddai, "The Almighty": Provision (91:1)
      3. Jehovah, "The Lord": Promise (91:2)
      4. Elohim, "God the Creator": Power (91:2)
   B. His Foes (91:3)
   C. His Faith (91:4)
II. IN TIMES OF TERROR (91:5–10)
III. IN TIMES OF TEMPTATION (91:11–16)
   A. A Triumphant Path (91:11–13)
   B. A Tremendous Promise (91:14–16)

PSALM 92

PRAISE THE SAVIOR, YE WHO KNOW HIM

I. THE EXCELLENCE OF PRAISE (92:1)
II. THE EXERCISE OF PRAISE (92:2)
    A. We Should Rest the Day with Him
    B. We Should Review the Day with Him
III. THE EXUBERANCE OF PRAISE (92:3)
    A. Praise Can Be Blissful
    B. Praise Must Be Balanced
IV. THE EXHAUSTLESSNESS OF PRAISE (92:4–5)
    A. The Things His Hands Have Performed (92:4–5a)
    B. The Things His Heart Has Planned (92:5b)
V. THE EXCEPTION TO PRAISE (92:6–7)
    A. The Insensitive Man (92:6)
    B. The Iniquitous Man (92:7)
VI. THE EXPLOSION OF PRAISE (92:8)
VII. THE EXPECTATION OF PRAISE (92:9–11)
    A. The Lord's Triumph Shown to the Psalmist (92:9)
    B. The Lord's Triumph Shared by the Psalmist (92:10–11)
VIII. THE EXPRESSION OF PRAISE (92:12–15)
    A. How Happy Are the Lord's People (92:12–14)
        1. The Fragrance of the Cedar (92:12)
        2. The Fruitfulness of the Psalm 92:13–14)
    B. How Holy Is the Lord's Person (92:15)

‿ PSALM 93 ‿

HE WHO STILLS THE STORM

IX. THE TIMES ARE HELD BY HIM (93:1–2)
    A. An Expression of the Full Sovereignty of God (93:1a)
    B. An Examination of the Fresh Stability of Earth (93:1b)
    C. An Exposure of the False Suppositions of Men (93:2)
X. THE TEMPEST IS HUSHED BY HIM (93:3–4)
    A. The Awesome Power of the Nations (93:3)
    B. The Actual Paralysis of the Nations (93:4)
XI. THE TEMPLE IS HOME TO HIM (93:5)
    A. Trust! The Law Is There (93:5a)
    B. Tremble! The Lord Is There (93:5b)

PSALM 94

THE AVENGER

I. THE SUPPLICATION (94:1–7)
  A. Hearken, Lord! (94:1–2)
    1. Vengeance Is Your Right (94:1)
    2. Vengeance Is Your Responsibility (94:2)
  B. Hasten, Lord! (94:3–7)
    1. The Heathen Demonstrate Their Power (94:3)
    2. The Heathen Declare Their Prowess (94:4)
    3. The Heathen Destroy Thy People (94:5–6)
    4. The Heathen Defame Thy Person (94:7)
II. THE SERMON (94:8–11)
  A. The Approach (94:8)
  B. The Appeal (94:9–10)
    1. God as Creator (94:9)
    2. God as Corrector (94:10a)
    3. God as Counselor (94:10b)
  C. The Application (94:11)
III. THE SOLILOQUY (94:12–23)
  A. The Psalmist Explores the Principles of God's Dealings (94:12–15)
    1. A Parental Aspect to God's Ways (94:12a)
    2. A Pedagogical Aspect to God's Ways (94:12b)

3. A Providential Aspect to God's Ways (94:13–14)
  a. God Provides a Period of Relief (94:13a)
  b. God Plans a Place of Retribution (94:13b)
  c. God Pursues a Policy of Reinstatement (94:14)
4. A Practical Aspect to God's Ways (94:15)
B. The Psalmist Experiences the Pleasure of God's Deliverance (94:16–19)
  1. His Case (94:16–17)
  2. His Cry (94:18)
  3. His Comfort (94:19)
C. The Psalmist Examines the Potential of God's Decisions (94:20–23)
  1. The Outraging of the Majesty of God (94:20–21)
  2. The Outpouring of the Mercy of God (94:22)
  3. The Outworking of the Morality of God (94:23)

PSALM 95

LEST HISTORY REPEAT ITSELF

I. PRAISING GOD (95:1–7)
   A. We Are Invited to Acclaim Him (95:1)
      1. His Name
      2. His Fame
   B. We Are Invited to Approach Him (95:2–5)
      1. In an Uninhibited Way (95:2)
         a. Gratefully
         b. Gladly
      2. In an Understanding Way (95:3–5)
         a. Mindful of God's Majesty (95:3)
         b. Mindful of God's Might (95:4–5)
   C. We Are Invited to Adore Him (95:6–7)
      1. Instinctively (95:6)
      2. Intelligently (95:7a)
      3. Instantly (95:7b)
II. PROVOKING GOD (95:8–11)
   A. The Sudden Crisis in Israel (95:8–9)
   B. The Settled Character of Israel (95:10)
   C. The Sad Consequence for Israel (95:11)

PSALM 96

LET US SING

I. ALL GLORY BELONGS TO GOD (96:1–6)
   A. What We Should Sing (96:1–2)
      1. We Should Sing a New Song (96:1)
      2. It Is a Necessary Song (96:2)
   B. Where We Should Sing (96:3)
   C. Why We Should Sing (96:4–6)
      Because of:
      1. The Fear of the Lord (96:4)
      2. The Fact of the Lord (96:5)
      3. The Fame of the Lord (96:6)

II. ALL GIFTS BELONG TO GOD (96:7–9)
   We should give of:
   A. Our Wonder (96:7–8a)
   B. Our Wealth (96:8b)
   C. Our Worship (96:9)

III. ALL GOVERNMENT BELONGS TO GOD (96:10–13)
   A. The Principles of the Coming Government (96:10)
      1. Absolute Sovereignty
      2. Absolute Security
      3. Absolute Sanctity
   B. The Prospect of the Coming Government (96:11–13)
      1. For All Nature (96:11–13a)
      2. For All Nations (96:13b)

PSALM 97

THE CROWNING DAY THAT'S COMING

I. THE LORD AS THE REIGNING ONE (97:1–9)
  A. The Ruler of All Nature (97:1–5)
    1. His Majesty's Sovereign Domains (97:1)
    2. His Majesty's Secret Dwelling (97:2)
    3. His Majesty's Strong Divisions (97:3–5)
  B. The Ruler of All Nations (97:6–9)
    1. The Heathen Peoples (97:6–7)
      a. The Truth Revealed (97:6)
      b. The Truth Received (97:7)
    2. The Hebrew People (97:8–9)
      a. Rejoicing in the Lord (97:8)
      b. Reveling in the Lord (97:9)
II. THE LORD AS THE RIGHTEOUS ONE (97:10–12)
  A. What the Lord Demands of His People (97:10)
  B. What the Lord Does for His People (97:11–12)
    1. He Fills Them with Light (97:11)
    2. He Fills Them with Laughter (97:12)

⟜ PSALM 98 ⟞

THE MAGNIFICAT OF THE OLD TESTAMENT

I. THE LORD'S MIGHT (98:1–2)
   A. The Song of the Lord (98:1–2)
   B. The Strength of the Lord (98:1b)
   C. The Salvation of the Lord (98:2)
II. THE LORD'S MERCY (98:3–6)
   A. The Remembrance of That Mercy (98:3)
   B. The Result of That Mercy (98:4–6)
III. THE LORD'S MAJESTY (98:7–9)
   A. The Jubilation of the Earth (98:7–9a)
   B. The Judgment of the Earth (98:9b)
      1. The Lord Will Rule Faithfully
      2. The Lord Will Rule Fairly

⌒ PSALM 99 ⌒

THE LAMB UPON HIS THRONE

I. THE IDEAL PRINCE (99:1–4)
  A. The Lord's Majesty (99:1–3)
    1. Exalted upon an Eternal Throne (99:1)
      a. The Goodness of God
      b. The Grace of God
      c. The Government of God
      d. The Glory of God
    2. Exalted Above All Earthly Thrones (99:2–3)
      a. How High He Is (99:2)
      b. How Holy He Is (99:3)
  B. The Lord's Morality (99:4)
    1. He Embraces Morality
    2. He Establishes Morality
    3. He Enforces Morality
II. THE IDEAL PRIEST (99:5–6)
  A. Worship Belongs to Him (99:5)
  B. Worship Brought to Him (99:6)
III. THE IDEAL PROPHET (99:7–9)
  A. His Message (99:7)
  B. His Mercy (99:8)
  C. His Ministry (99:9)

—•—

PSALM 100

A UNIVERSAL HYMN OF PRAISE

I. APPROACHING GOD (100:1–2)
  A. Unrivaled Harmony (100:1)
  B. Unrestrained Happiness (100:2)
II. APPREHENDING GOD (100:3)
  A. His Person
  B. His Power
  C. His Purpose
III. APPRECIATING GOD (100:4–5)
  A. Coming to Him—Thankfully (100:4)
    1. Arriving at the Temple
    2. Arriving at the Truth
  B. Communing with Him—Thoughtfully (100:5)
    1. An Essential Fact (God's Goodness)
    2. An Eternal Fact (God's Mercy)
    3. An Enduring Fact (God's Truth)

⟨PSALM 101⟩

A KING'S RESOLVES

I. THE KING AND HIS CHARACTER (101:1–2)
A. His Delight (101:1)
B. His Decision (101:2a)
C. His Desire (101:2b)
D. His Dwelling (101:2c)
II. THE KING AND HIS COUNTRYMEN (101:3–5)
A. Holiness Through Sanctification (101:3)
B. Holiness Through Separation (101:4)
C. Holiness Through Severity (101:5)
III. THE KING AND HIS COURTIERS (101:6–8)
A. The Counselors He Wants (101:6)
1. Men to Reside with Him
2. Men to Reign with Him
B. The Convictions He Wants (101:7–8)
1. His Personal Resolve (101:7)
2. His Public Resolve (101:8)

⁀PSALM 102⁀

AMIDST THE ENCIRCLING GLOOM

I. A REALLY GLOOMY SITUATION (102:1–11)
   A. The Psalmist's Cry (102:1–2)
   B. The Psalmist's Condition (102:3–11)
      1. His Endurance Is Gone (102:3–5)
         a. His Days Are Consumed by Fire (102:3)
         b. His Desire Is Consumed by Fasts (102:4–5)
      2. His Environment Is Wrong (102:6–7)
      3. His Enemy Is Strong (102:8–11)
         a. The Greatness of Their Scorn (102:8)
         b. The Grounds for Their Scorn (102:9–11)
II. A REMARKABLY GOLDEN SUNBEAM (102:12–22)
   A. A Dawning Hope (102:12–17)
      1. God Will Remember Zion (102:12–14)
         a. The Truth Factor (102:12)
         b. The Time Factor (102:13)
         c. The Testimony Factor (102:14)
      2. God Will Rebuild Zion (102:15–17)
         a. The Reality of It (102:15–16)
         b. The Reason for It (102:17)
   B. A Distant Hope (102:18–22)
      1. A Future People (102:18–20)
      2. A Future Prospect (102:21–22)

III. A RETURNING GRAY SKY (102:23–28)
   A. His Remaining Fear (102:23–24a)
   B. His Rising Faith (102:24b–28)
      1. You Are a Timeless God (102:24b)
      2. You Are a Tremendous God (102:25–27)
         a. Immeasurable in Power (102:25)
         b. Immutable in Person (102:26–27)
      3. You Are a Trustworthy God (102:28)

THE SONG OF A SOUL SET FREE

I. GOD'S MAN (103:1–7)
   A. The Penitent (103:3)
   B. The Patient (103:3)
   C. The Pauper (103:4)
   D. The Prince (103:4)
   E. The Pensioner (103:5)
II. GOD'S MERCY (103:8–18)
   A. He Manifests His Mercy (103:8–10)
   B. He Measures His Mercy (103:11–12)
   C. He Multiplies His Mercy (103:13–16)
   D. He Maintains His Mercy (103:17–18)
III. GOD'S MIGHT (103:19–22)
   A. The Heavenly Throne (103:19)
   B. The Heavenly Throng (103:20–22)

PSALM 104

A POEM OF CREATION

I. THE GLORY OF GOD'S PERSON (104:1)
   A. An Instinctive Word of Worship (104:1a)
   B. An Intelligent Word of Worship (104:1b)
II. THE GLORY OF GOD'S POWER (104:2–31)
   A. The Foundation Work of Creation (104:2–9)
      1. The Realm of the Skies Above Us (104:2–4)
         a. The Astral Heavens (104:2)
         b. The Atmospheric Heavens (104:3)
         c. The Angelic Heavens (104:4)
      2. The Realm of the Seas Around Us (104:5–9)
         a. Setting the Boundaries of the Sea's Reach (104:5–8)
         b. Setting the Boundaries of the Sea's Rage (104:9)
   B. The Further Works of Creation (104:10–30)
      1. A Beautiful Scene (104:10–18)
         a. The Running Waters (104:10–13)
         b. The Rolling Hills (104:14–17)
         c. The Rising Peaks (104:18)

PSALM 105

How Good Is the God We Adore

I. ISRAEL'S EXHORTATION (105:1–6)
A. A Call to Rejoice (105:1–2)
B. A Call to Return (105:3–4)
C. A Call to Remember (105:5–6)
II. ISRAEL'S EXPECTATION (105:7–15)
A. How God Decreed the Provisions of the Covenant (105:7–11)
1. How Sovereign God Is (105:7)
2. How Sincere God Is (105:8)
3. How Selective God Is (105:9–10)
4. How Specific God Is (105:11)
B. How God Delivered the People of the Covenant (105:12–15)
1. A Paltry People (105:12)
2. A Pilgrim People (105:13)
3. A Protected People (105:14–15)
III. ISRAEL'S EXILE (105:16–25)
A. Joseph in Egypt (105:16–22)
1. The Divine Purpose (105:16)
2. The Divine Process (105:17–22)
B. Jacob in Egypt (105:23–25)
1. Jacob's Descent into Egypt (105:23)
2. Jacob's Descendants in Egypt (105:24–25)

IV. ISRAEL'S EXODUS (105:26–38)
   A. The Men Involved (105:26)
   B. The Miracles Involved (105:27–36)
      1. Their Purpose (105:27)
      2. Their Particulars (105:28–36)
         a. Plagues That Filled the Egyptians with Doubt (105:28–29)
         b. Plagues That Filled the Egyptians with Disgust (105:30–31)
         c. Plagues That Filled the Egyptians with Dread (105:32–33)
         d. Plagues That Filled the Egyptians with Dismay (105:34–35)
         e. Plagues That Filled the Egyptians with Despair (105:36)
   C. The Mandate Involved (105:37–38)
V. ISRAEL'S EXPERIENCES (105:39–41)
   A. How God Led His People (105:39)
   B. How God Fed His People (105:40–41)
VI. ISRAEL'S EXALTATION (105:42–45)
   A. The Lord Was Gracious to Israel (105:42–43)
      1. He Remembered His Promise (105:42)
      2. He Redeemed His Promise (105:43)
   B. The Land Was Given to Israel (105:44–45)
      1. The Remarkable Provision (105:44)
      2. The Real Purpose (105:45)

⌒PSALM 106⌒

NATIONAL CONFESSION

I. A SOUND HEART (106:1–6)
   A. An Exciting Note of Praise (106:1–3)
      1. Remembering the Lord's Person (106:1a)
      2. Remembering the Lord's Pity (106:1b)
      3. Remembering the Lord's Power (106:2)
      4. Remembering the Lord's People (106:3)
   B. An Explicit Need for Prayer (106:4–6)
      1. The Psalmist's Concern (106:4–5)
      2. The Psalmist's Confession (106:6)
II. A SAD HISTORY (106:7–46)
   A. Natural Blindness in the Place of Bondage—Egypt (106:7–12)
      1. Ungrateful Grumbling (106:7)
      2. Unstinted Grace (106:8–11)
      3. Unrestrained Gladness (106:12)
   B. Negative Behavior in the Place of Barrenness—the Wilderness (106:13–33)
      1. Their Lustful Desires (106:13–15)
      2. Their Lawless Demands (106:16–18)
      3. Their Lying Dogmas (106:19–27)
         a. Unbelief Regarding the Lord (106:19–23)
         b. Unbelief Regarding the Land (106:24–27)
      4. Their Loathsome Deeds (106:28–31)
      5. Their Lasting Distrust (106:32–33)

C. Near Blasphemy in the Place of Blessing-the Land
   (106:34–46)
   1. The Fatal Seed (106:34)
   2. The Fearful Weed (106:35–39)
      a. The Deeds of the Heathen Acclaimed 106:35)
      b. The Creeds of the Heathen Accepted (106:35–39)
   3. The Final Need (106:40–46)
III. A SURE HOPE (106:47–48)
   A. The Blessing (106:47)
      1. May God End Their Exile (106:47a)
      2. May God Ensure Their Exaltation (106:47b)
   B. The Benediction (106:48)

———•———

PSALM 107

THE SONG OF A SOUL SET FREE

I. HOW GOD REGATHERED THE SCATTERED AND
REJECTED PEOPLE OF ISRAEL (107:1–3)
A. What the Lord Deserves (107:1)
B. What the Lord Did (107:2–3)

II. HOW GOD REGARDED THE SPIRITUAL AND
REAL PLIGHT OF ISRAEL (107:4–32)
Israel was like:
A. A Person Lost in the Desert (107:4–9)
B. A Person Locked in a Dungeon (107:10–16)
C. A Person Lying on a Deathbed (107:17–22)
D. A Person Lashed on the Deep (107:23–32)

III. HOW GOD RESTORED THE SCARRED AND
RUINED PROPERTY OF ISRAEL (107:33–38)
A. The Land Made Barren (107:33–34)
B. The Land Made Beautiful (107:35–38)

IV. HOW GOD REVIVED THE SOCIAL AND RELIGIOUS
PROSPERITY OF ISRAEL (107:39–43)
A. The Sadness of Israel's Judgment (107:39–40)
B. The Success of Israel's Judgment (107:41–43)

PSALM 108

TELL ME THE OLD, OLD STORY

I. MUSIC (108:1–3)
  A. The Inspiration of Praise (108:1)
  B. The Instruments of Praise (108:2a)
  C. The Insistence of Praise (108:2b)
  D. The Infectiousness of Praise (108:3)
II. MAJESTY (108:4–6)
  God is:
  A. Majestic in His Government (108:4)
  B. Majestic in His Glory (108:5)
  C. Majestic in His Grace (108:6)
III. MIGHT (108:7–11)
  A. The Basic Facts (108:7–8)
    1. "These are My plans"—I will… I will…
    2. "These are My people"—Mine… Mine…
    3. "These are My prerogatives"—Ephraim is…
       Judah is…
  B. The Beaten Foes (108:9)
  C. The Beloved Friend (108:10–11)
    1. An Impossible Task (108:10)
    2. An Important Truth (108:11)
IV. MERCY (108:12–13)
  A. A Realistic Assessment (108:12)
  B. A Real Assurance (108:13)

PSALM 109

LET HIM BE ACCURSED

I. DAVID'S FAITH EXERCISED (109:1–5)
   A. The Divine Attention He Sought (109:1)
   B. The Deadly Attack He Fought (109:2–3)
   C. The Devout Attitude He Taught (109:4–5)
II. DAVID'S FOES EXPOSED (109:6–19)
   A. An Appalling Curse (109:6–15)
   That David might be the victim of:
   1. Spiritual Infamy (109:6)
   2. Social Injustice (109:7a)
   3. Startling Iniquity (109:7b)
   4. Serious Injury (109:8–9)
   5. Stifling Insolvency (109:10–11)
   6. Sordid Inhumanity (109:12)
   7. Sudden Infertility (109:13)
   8. Solemn Invective (109:14–15)
   B. An Appended Claim (109:16–19)
   David, supposedly, was:
   1. Addicted to Cruelty (109:16)
   2. Addicted to Cursing (109:17–19)
III. DAVID'S FEARS EXPRESSED (109:20–31)
   A. O Lord, Remember My Cursers (109:20)
   B. O Lord, Remember My Condition (109:21–25)
   1. Please Be Mindful of Your Mercy (109:21)
   2. Please Be Mindful of My Misery (109:22–25)
   C. O Lord, Remember My Cause (109:26–31)
   1. Let My Assurance Be Vindicated (109:26–27)
   2. Let My Assailants Be Vanquished (109:28–31)

PSALM 110

THE MELCHIZEDEK PSALM

I. THE MESSIANIC PRINCE (110:1–3)
  A. His Remarkable Position (110:1)
  B. His Resistless Power (110:2)
  C. His Redeemed People (110:3)
II. THE MELCHIZEDEK PRIEST (110:4)
  A. The Divine Oath
  B. The Durable Office
  C. The Distinctive Order
    1. A Stable Priesthood
    2. A Sovereign Priesthood
    3. A Superior Priesthood
III. THE MILLENNIAL PROPHECY (110:5–7)
  A. The Day of Battle (110:5)
  B. The Din of Battle (110:6)
  C. The Dust of Battle (110:7)

THE LORD'S WORKS

I. WORSHIP (111:1–3)
   A. The Resolve to Worship (111:1)
      1. Personally
      2. Publicly
   B. The Reasons for Worship (111:2–3)
      1. God's Might Displayed (111:2)
      2. God's Majesty Displayed (111:3)
II. WONDER (111:4–6)
   A. Apprehending What He Has Done (111:4)
   B. Appreciating What He Has Done (111:5)
      1. God's Faithfulness to His Creatures
      2. God's Faithfulness to His Covenant
   C. Appropriating What He Has Done (111:6)
III. WISDOM (111:7–10)
   A. Fresh Regard for the Lord (111:7–9)
      1. His Work Is Guaranteed by His Nature (111:7–8)
      2. His Works Are Guaranteed by His Name (111:9)
   B. Fresh Response to the Lord (111:10)
      1. Where Wisdom Starts
      2. Why Wisdom Stands
      3. When Wisdom Sings

PSALM 112

THE BLESSED MAN

I. THE SECRET OF THE BLESSED MAN (112:1)
   A. He Loves the Lord
   B. He Loves the Word

II. THE SONS OF THE BLESSED MAN (112:2)
   A. They Are Mighty Men
   B. They Are Moral Men

III. THE SUBSTANCE OF THE BLESSED MAN (112:3)
   He has:
   A. A House Full of Riches
   B. A Heart Full of Righteousness

IV. THE SERENITY OF THE BLESSED MAN (112:4)
   He enjoys:
   A. Guidance
   B. Grace
   C. Goodness
   D. Godliness

V. THE SENSE OF THE BLESSED MAN (112:5)
   A. He Is Compassionate
   B. He Is Careful

VI. THE SECURITY OF THE BLESSED MAN (112:6–8)
   A. His Is an Everlasting Security (112:6)
   B. His Is an Everyday Security (112:7–8)
      1. Bad News Does Not Shake Him (112:7)
      2. Good News Does Not Shun Him (112:8)

VII. THE STATUS OF THE BLESSED MAN (112:9)
   A. His Pity Is Acknowledged
   B. His Piety Is Acknowledged
   C. His Power Is Acknowledged
VIII. THE SUPREMACY OF THE BLESSED MAN (112:10)
   He sees:
   A. The Frustration of the Wicked
   B. The Fury of the Wicked
   C. The Folly of the Wicked

———•———

PSALM 113

HALLELUJAH!

I.   THE LORD DEMANDS PRAISE (113:1–3)
    A. His Rightful Claim (113:1a–b)
    B. His Royal Name (113:1c–2)
    C. His Resounding Fame (113:3)
II. THE LORD DESIRES PRAISE (113:4–6)
    A. His Glory (113:4)
    B. His Greatness (113:5)
    C. His Grace (113:6)
III. THE LORD DESERVES PRAISE (113:7–9)
    A. His Kindness to the Downtrodden (113:7–8)
       He brings them:
       1. Up from the Pit (113:7)
       2. Into the Palace (113:8)
    B. His Kindness to the Distressed (113:9)

PSALM 114

HOW GOD GIVES POWER

I. THE ROOTS OF SPIRITUAL POWER (114:1–2)
   A. Separation (114:1)
   B. Sanctification (114:2a)
   C. Surrender (114:2b)
II. THE RESULTS OF SPIRITUAL POWER (114:3–8)
   A. Things Begin to Happen (114:3–6)
      1. We Are Invincible (114:3–4)
         a. Obstacles Will Be Removed (114:3)
         b. Opportunities Will Be Revealed (114:4)
      2. We Are Invulnerable (114:5–6)
   B. Throngs Begin to Hearken (114:7–8)
      1. Conviction (114:7)
      2. Conversion (114:8)

⁕PSALM 115⁕

IDOLATRY EXPOSED

III. APPRECIATION (115:1–3)
   A. Sanctity of God's Name (115:1)
   B. Scoffers of God's Fame (115:2)
   C. Straightness of God's Aim (115:3)
IV. APPRAISAL (115:4–8)
   A. Form of the Idol (115:4–7)
   B. Folly of the Idolator (115:8)
V. APPEAL (115:9–11)
   A. Covenant People (115:9)
   B. Consecrated Priest (115:10)
   C. Converted Pagan (115:11)
VI. APPLICATION (115:12–15)
   A. Assurance of the Blessing (115:12–13)
   B. Assessment of the Blessing (115:14–15)
VII. APPLAUSE (115:16–18)
   A. The Globe (115:16)
   B. The Grave (115:17)
   C. The Godly (115:18)

PSALM 116

THANK YOU, LORD!

VIII. THE PSALMIST'S GRATITUDE (116:1–9)
  A. The Danger He Experienced (116:1–4)
    1. His Present Assurance (116:1–2)
    2. His Previous Anguish (116:3)
    3. His Prayerful Appeal (116:4)
  B. The Deliverance He Experienced (116:5–9)
    1. A Word About His Savior (116:5–6)
    2. A Word to His Soul (116:7–9)
IX. THE PSALMIST'S GRIEF (116:10–11)
  A. What He Had Suffered (116:10)
  B. What He Had Said (116:11)
X. THE PSALMIST'S GOALS (116:12–15)
  A. His Assessment of His Duty (116:12–14)
  B. His Assurance About His Death (116:15)
XI. THE PSALMIST'S GLADNESS (116:16–19)
  A. His Position (116:16)
  B. His Promise (116:17–19)
    1. To Live a Sacrificial Life (116:17)
    2. To Live a Sanctified Life (116:18–19)

PSALM 117

INTERNATIONAL PRAISE

PSALM 118

THE JOURNEY HOME

I. COMMENCEMENT OF THE JOURNEY (118:1–4)
   A. The Worshiper's Theme (118:1)
   B. The Worshiping Throng (118:2–4)

II. CHARACTER OF THE JOURNEY (118:5–18)
   A. At Gethsemane (118:5–7)
      1. The Prayer That Was Answered (118:5)
      2. The Peace That Was Assured (118:6)
      3. The Presence That Was Alongside (118:7)
   B. At Gabbatha (118:8–9)
   C. At Golgotha (118:10–13)
      1. The Human Foes (118:10–12)
      2. The Hidden Foe (118:13)
   D. In Glory (118:14–18)
      1. Rejoicing in His Redeemed People (118:14–16)
      2. Rejoicing in His Resurrection Power (118:17–18)

III. CLIMAX OF THE JOURNEY (118:19–29)
   A. The Lord Jesus at the Portals of the Temple (118:19–26)
      1. The Simple Prayer (118:19–21)
      2. The Sudden Pause (118:22–23)
      3. The Sounding Praise (118:24–26)
   B. The Lord Jesus in the Precincts of the Temple (118:27–29)
      1. The Coming Sacrifice (118:27)
      2. The Coming Song (118:28–29)

PSALM 119:1–8

SING A SONG OF SCRIPTURE

The Bible will make:

I. A HAPPY MAN (119:1–3)
   A. In His Way (119:1a)
   B. In His Walk (119:1b)
   C. In His Will (119:2–3)
      1. Gives Purpose to Life (119:2)
      2. Guarantees Purity in Life (119:3)
II. A HOLY MAN (119:4–6)
   A. His Duty (119:4)
   B. His Desire (119:5)
   C. His Decision (119:6)
III. A HUMBLE MAN (119:7–8)
   A. Still Learning (119:7)
   B. Still Longing (119:8)

PSALM 119:9–16

GOD'S WORD HID IN THE HEART

I. THE VIRTUE OF THE WORD (119:9–16)
   A. Its Cleansing Effect (119:9)
   B. Its Controlling Effect (119:10)
   C. Its Correcting Effect (119:11–12)
II. THE VALUE OF THE WORD (119:13–16)
   A. We Must Proclaim It (119:13)
      1. The Need for Diligence (119:13a)
      2. The Need for Daring (119:13b)
   B. We Must Prize It (119:14–15)
      1. Its Priceless Worth (119:14)
      2. Its Practical Worth (119:15)
   C. We Must Prove It (119:16)

PSALM 119:17–24

WONDROUS THINGS OUT OF THY LAW

I. FINDING GREAT OPPORTUNITIES IN
    THE WORD OF GOD (119:17–20)
    A. It Bestows Life on the Soul (119:17)
    B. It Brings Light into the Soul (119:18)
    C. It Banishes Loneliness from the Soul (119:19)
    D. It Bares Longings in the Soul (119:20)
II. FINDING GREAT OPPOSITION TO THE
    WORD OF GOD (119:21–24)
    A. The Antipathy (119:21–23)
        1. The Domineering Man, Cursed of God (119:21)
        2. The Disdainful Man, Contemptuous of God (119:22)
        3. The Dangerous Man, Controlled by God (119:23)
    B. The Antidote (119:24)

PSALM 119:25–32

GLEAMS AMID THE GLOOM

I. WHAT THE PSALMIST REALIZED (119:25–29)
   God's Word:
   A. In Conviction (119:25)
   B. In Confession (119:26)
   C. In Consecration (119:27)
   D. In Contrition (119:28)
   E. In Contrast (119:29)
II. WHAT THE PSALMIST RESOLVED (119:30–32)
   A. His Decision to Live for God (119:30)
   B. His Determination to Live for God (119:31)
   C. His Desire to Live for God (119:32)

PSALM 119:33–40

FOUR PICTURES OF A MAN OF GOD

I. SOJOURNER (119:33–34)
   He promises to follow God's direction:
   A. Faithfully (119:33)
   B. Fully (119:34)
II. SOLDIER (119:35–36)
   He underlines:
   A. The Discipline Needed (119:35)
   B. The Desire Needed (119.36)
III. SERVANT (119:37–38)
   A. A Discerning Servant (119:37)
   B. A Devoted Servant (119:38)
IV. SAINT (119:39–40)
   He wanted to be:
   A. A Good Man (119:39)
   B. A Godly Man (119:40)

☞ PSALM 119:41-48 ☜

FLASHES OF LIGHT FROM GOD'S WORD

The psalmist wants to:
I.   EXPERIENCE THE PROTECTION
      OF GOD'S WORD (119:41)
II.   EXERCISE THE POWER OF GOD'S WORD (119:42)
III. EXPRESS THE PROOF OF GOD'S WORD (119:43)
IV.   EXPLAIN THE PERMANENCE OF GOD'S WORD (119:44)
V.   EXPLORE THE PATH OF GOD'S WORD (119:45)
VI.   EXPOUND THE PRINCIPLES OF GOD'S WORD (119:46)
VII. EXTRACT THE PLEASURES OF GOD'S WORD (119:47)
VIII. EXAMINE THE POTENTIAL OF GOD'S WORD (119:48)

PSALM 119:49–56

HOPE

I. WHAT THE PSALMIST REQUESTED (119:49)
II. WHAT THE PSALMIST RECOGNIZED (119:50–51)
God's Word was:
  A. Life to Him When Injured (119:50)
  B. Law to Him When Insulted (119:51)
III. WHAT THE PSALMIST REMEMBERED (119:52–56)
  A. The Lord's Nature (119:52–54)
    1. It Comforted Him (119:52)
    2. It Consoled Him (119:53–54)
  B. The Lord's Name (119:55–56)
  It had:
    1. Become Precious to Him (119:55)
    2. Become Part of Him (119:56)

144

PSALM 119:57-64

RUINED BUT STILL REJOICING

I. THE PSALMIST'S FIND (119:57–58)
   A. What He Realized (119:57a)
   B. What He Resolved (119:57b)
   C. What He Requested (119:58)
II. THE PSALMIST'S FEET (119:59–60)
   Directed in the way of:
   A. Perfect Obedience (119:59)
   B. Prompt Obedience (119:60)
III. THE PSALMIST'S FOES (119:61)
IV. THE PSALMIST'S FERVOR (119:62)
V. THE PSALMIST'S FRIENDS (119:63)
VI. THE PSALMIST'S FACTS (119:64)
   A. What He Discovered (119:64a)
   B. What He Desired (119:64b)

PSALM 119:65–72

It Is Well with My Soul

I. THE PSALMIST'S WORD OF TESTIMONY (119:65)
II. THE PSALMIST'S WISH FOR TEACHING (119:66–68)
   A. What He Expressed (119:66)
   B. What He Experienced (119:67)
   C. What He Expected (119:68)
III. THE PSALMIST'S WAY IN TESTING (119:69–71)
   A. His Reaction to Those Who Affronted Him (119:69–70)
     1. To Their Sneers (119:69)
     2. To Their Smugness (119:70)
   B. His Reaction to That Which Afflicted Him (119:71)
IV. THE PSALMIST'S WEALTH OF TREASURE (119:72)

PSALM 119:73–80

IN GOOD COMPANY

I. THE LORD'S HAND (119:73–75)
    A. In Making Him (119:73)
       He was sure the Lord had:
       1. A Part in Making Him
       2. A Purpose in Making Him
    B. In Motivating Him (119:74)
    C. In Molding Him (119:75)
II. THE LORD'S HEART (119:76–77)
    He wanted the Lord to:
    A. Show His Love to Him (119:76)
    B. Share His Love with Him (119:77)
III. THE LORD'S HELP (119:78–80)
    He wanted to be:
    A. Successful in the Fight (119:78)
    B. Secure in the Fellowship (119:79)
    C. Sound in the Faith (119:80)

PSALM 119:81–88

A Bottle in the Smoke

I.   A TROUBLED SOUL (119:81–83)
   A. He Needed Revival (119:81–82)
      1. His Soul Was Fainting—-Longing for a Work of God (119:81)
      2. His Sight Was Failing—Looking for a Word from God (119:82)
   B. He Needed Restoration (119:83)
II. A TRYING SITUATION (119:84–87)
   He is faced with:
      1. Seeming Delay (119:84)
      2. Systematic Deceit (119:85)
      3. Serious Danger (119:86–87)
         a. What He Sought (119:86)
         b. What He Survived (119:87)
III. A TRUSTING SAINT (119:88)

PSALM 119:89–96

SETTLED IN HEAVEN

I. THE PERMANENCE OF GOD'S WORD (119:89–91)
A. Why (119:89a)
B. Where (119:89b–90)
1. In the Glory (119:89b)
2. On This Globe (119:90)
C. When (119:91)
II. THE PROTECTION OF GOD'S WORD (119:92)
III. THE POWER OF GOD'S WORD (119:93–95)
A. To Save Him (119:93–94)
How it:
1. Quickened His Faith (119:93)
2. Quelled His Foes (119:94)
B. To Safeguard Him (119:95)
IV. THE PERFECTION OF GOD'S WORD (119:96)

PSALM 119:97–104

A Scholar and a Saint

I. THE SOURCE OF TRUE SCHOLARSHIP (119:97–100)
    A. The Glorious Occupation of the Psalmist (119:97)
    B. The Glorious Outcome for the Psalmist (119:98–100)
       A mind sharpened by the Word of God is better than wits sharpened by:
       1. Enmity (119:98)
       2. Education (119:99)
       3. Experience (119:100)
II. THE SOURCE OF TRUE SANCTITY (119:101–104)
    A. A Separated Life (119:101)
    B. A Steadfast Life (119:102)
    C. A Satisfied Life (119:103)
    D. A Sterling Life (119:104)

PSALM 119:105–112

THE LAMP

I. GOD'S WORD GUIDES US (119:105–108)
   A. In Our Walk (119:105–106)
      1. The Way Found (119:105)
      2. The Way Followed (119:106)
   B. In Our Weakness (119:107)
   C. In Our Worship (119:108)
II. GOD'S WORD GUARDS US (119:109–110)
   A. Hushes Our Fears (119:109)
   B. Hinders Our Foes (119:110)
III. GOD'S WORD GLADDENS US (119:111–112)
   It will remind us of:
   A. Our Happy Heritage (119:111)
   B. Our Heavenly Home (119:112)

PSALM 119:113–120

TRUSTING AND TREMBLING

I. WHOM THE PSALMIST TRUSTED (119:113–117)
   A. His Vacillation Is Assessed (119:113)
   B. His Victory Is Assured (119:114)
   C. His Virtue Is Assailed (119:115–117)
      He expresses his need for:
      1. Separation (119:115)
      2. Scripture (119:116)
      3. Support (119:117)
II. WHY THE PSALMIST TREMBLED (119:118–120)
   A. At the Justice of God (119:118–119)
      1. In His Dealings with the Wayward (119:118)
      2. In His Dealings with the Wicked (119:119)
   B. At the Judgment of God (119:120)

PSALM 119:121–128

LORD, IT IS TIME

I. HIS SERIOUS CONCERN (119:121–124)
    He wanted God to act:
    A. In Government (119:121)
    B. As Guarantor (119:122)
    C. With Grace (119:123–124)
       1. Saving Him (119:123)
       2. Strengthening Him (119:124)
II. HIS SWEET CAPTIVITY (119:125)
III. HIS SOLE COMPLAINT (119:126)
    A. How Daring He Was (119:126a)
    B. How Discerning He Was (119:126b)
IV. HIS SIGNIFICANT CLAIM (119:127–128)
    A. The Treasure He Loved (119:127)
    B. The Truth He Lived (119:128)

GOD'S WONDERFUL WORD

I. THE PSALMIST AS TRIUMPHANT (119:129–131)
   A. Living by God's Word (119:129)
   B. Lighted by God's Word (119:130)
   C. Longing for God's Word (119:131)
II. THE PSALMIST AS TREMBLING (119:132–136)
   A. Distance Is Sensed (119:132)
   B. Direction Is Sought (119:133)
   C. Deliverance Is Supplicated (119:134)
   D. Darkness Is Scattered (119:135)
   E. Disaster Is Seen (119:186)

PSALM 119:137–144

GOD'S WORD IS RIGHT

I. THE PSALMIST'S DISCERNMENT (119:137–138)
   The righteousness of:
   A. The Lord's Character (119:137)
   B. The Lord's Commandments (119:138)
II. THE PSALMIST'S DEVOTION (119:139)
III. THE PSALMIST'S DELIGHT (119:140)
IV. THE PSALMIST'S DISTRESS (119:141–143)
   A. His Correct View of Self (119:141)
   B. His Correct View of Scripture (119:142)
   C. His Correct View of Suffering (119:143)
V. THE PSALMIST'S DESIRE (119:144)

CRYING WITH THE WHOLE HEART

I. THE PSALMIST CRYING (119:145–148)
   A. How Fervent He Was (119:145)
   B. How Frustrated He Was (119:146)
   C. How Forward He Was (119:147–148)
      1. Praying Before Rising in the Morning (119:147)
      2. Praying Before Retiring in the Evening (119:148)
II. THE PSALMIST CALLING (119:149–151)
   A. His Simple Plea Is Described (119:149)
   B. His Sudden Plight Is Described (119:150)
   C. His Safe Place Is Described (119:151)
III. THE PSALMIST CONFESSING (119:152)

PSALM 119:153–160

WHEN AFFLICTION COMES

I. THE PSALMIST'S ASSESSMENT (119:153–156)
   A. His Situation (119:153–155)
      It made him:
      1. More Thoughtful in Prayer (119:153–154)
         He opens his life to:
         a. God's Inspection (119:153)
         b. God's Intervention (119:154)
      2. More Thankful in Prayer (119:155)
   B. His Savior (119:156)
II. THE PSALMIST'S ASSAILANTS (119:157–158)
   He was:
   A. Troubled by Their Attacks (119:157)
   B. Troubled by Their Attitude (119:158)
III. THE PSALMIST'S ASSURANCE (119:159–160)
   A. His Devotion to God's Word (119:159)
   B. His Discernment of God's Word (119:160)

PSALM 119:161–168

PEACE IN SPITE OF PERSECUTION

I. THE PERSECUTED MAN (119:161)
II. THE PRAISING MAN (119:162–164)
   A. What He Discovered (119:162)
   B. What He Detested (119:163)
   C. What He Did (119:164)
III. THE PEACEFUL MAN (119:165)
IV. THE PATIENT MAN (119:166)
V. THE PASSIONATE MAN (119:167)
VI. THE PERFECT MAN (119:168)

⌒PSALM 119:169–176⌒

A FINAL PLEA

I. LORD, HEAR ME (119:169–172)
  A. The Prayer (119:169–170)
    1. For Enlightenment (119:169)
    2. For Enablement (119:170)
  B. The Promise (119:171–172)
    1. He Would Praise the Lord (119:171)
    2. He Would Proclaim the Word (119:172)

II. LORD, HELP ME (119:173–176)
  A. Lord, Save Me (119:173)
    1. The Ground of the Appeal
    2. The Greatness of the Appeal
  B. Lord, Satisfy Me (119:174)
  C. Lord, Strengthen Me (119:175)
  He wanted something:
    1. Wrought in Him
    2. Brought from Him
    3. Taught to Him
  D. Lord, Seek Me (119:176)
  We see him:
    1. Straying
    2. Praying

THE WAR LORDS

I. THE PSALMIST'S DISTRESS (120:1)
II. THE PSALMIST'S DECEIVERS (120:2–4)
  A. What He Wanted (120:2)
  B. What He Wondered (120:3)
  C. What He Wished (120:4)
III. THE PSALMIST'S DWELLING (120:5)
IV. THE PSALMIST'S DESIRE (120:6–7)
  A. The Warlike Atmosphere by Which He Was Surrounded (120:6)
  B. The Wonderful Attitude by Which He Was Sustained (120:7)

PSALM 121

SAFE IN THE ARMS OF JESUS

I. THE LORD IS MY KING (121:1–2)
   A. The Awe-Inspiring Hills (121:1a)
   B. The All-Sufficient Helper (121:2)
II. THE LORD IS MY KEEPER (121:3–8)
   He takes care of:
   A. The Problem of Weariness (121:3–4)
      He knows how easy it is for me:
      1. To Slip (121:3a)
      2. To Sleep (121:3b–4)
   B. The Problem of Weakness (121:5–6)
      I am vulnerable:
      1. On All Sides (121:5)
      2. At All Seasons (121:6)
   C. The Problem of Wickedness (121:7)
   D. The Problem of Waywardness (121:8)

PSALM 122

JERUSALEM! JERUSALEM!

I. A SURGE OF HAPPINESS AT THE SIGHT
OF JERUSALEM (122:1–3)
A. A Word of Delight (122:1)
B. A Word of Determination (122:2)
C. A Word of Description (122:3)
II. A SOURCE OF HOLINESS IN THE STREETS
OF JERUSALEM (122:4–5)
A. Holiness Is Encouraged: Spiritual Power Was Evident
(122:4)
B. Holiness Is Enforced: Secular Power Was Evident (122:5)
III. A SENSE OF HEAVINESS AT THE STRESS
OF JERUSALEM (122:6–9)
A. Request for Prayer for Jerusalem (122:6a)
B. Reasons for Praying for Jerusalem (122:6b–9)
Praying for Jerusalem will prove to be:
1. A Blessing (122:6b)
2. A Bulwark (122:7–9)

PSALM 123

SCORNED

PSALM 124

ESCAPED

I. RECOGNITION OF THE LORD'S PRESENCE (124:1–2)
   A. The Double Declaration (124:1–2a)
   B. The Deadly Danger (124:2b)
II. RECOGNITION OF THE LORD'S PROTECTION (124:3–5)
   A. From Being Devoured (124:3)
   B. From Being Drowned (124:4–5)
III. RECOGNITION OF THE LORD'S PREEMINENCE (124:6–8)
   A. Blessing the Name of the Lord (124:6–7)
      1. For Hindering (124:6)
      2. For Helping (124:7)
   B. Broadcasting the Fame of the Lord (124:8)

PSALM 125

SAFE

I. THE VICTORIOUS SAINT (125:1–4)
  A. Safe as to His Person (125:1–2)
    1. The Essential Security of the Believer (125:1)
    2. The Eternal Security of the Believer (125:2)
  B. Safe as to His Possessions (125:3–4)
    1. The Problem (125:3)
    2. The Prayer (125:4)
II. THE VANQUISHED SINNER (125:5)
  A. His Crooked Dealings (125:5a)
  B. His Coming Downfall (125:5b)
III. THE VIRTUOUS SIGH (125:5c)

PSALM 126

FREE AT LAST

⮞ PSALM 127 ⮜

BUILDING HOUSE AND HOME

I. A PROPER SENSE OF VANITY (127:1–2)
   A. Working in Vain (127:1a)
   B. Watching in Vain (127:1b)
   C. Worrying in Vain (127:2)
II. A PROPER SENSE OF VALUES (127:3–5)
   Children are:
   A. Our Heritage (127:3)
   B. Our Helpers (127:4)
   C. Our Happiness (127:5)

THE WELLBEING OF HOME AND NATION

I. THE SANCTITY OF OUR HOME LIFE (128:1–4)
   A. The Secret of the Lord's Blessing (128:1)
      1. A Proper Center: the Lord (128:1a)
      2. A Proper Circumference: the Law (128:1b)
   B. The Scope of the Lord's Blessing (128:2–3)
     He will take care of:
      1. Our Finances (128:2a)
      2. Our Feelings (128:2b)
      3. Our Future (128:2c)
      4. Our Family (128:3)
   C. The Surety of the Lord's Blessing (128:4)
II. THE SECURITY OF OUR HOME LAND (128:5–6)
   A. Security at the Center (128:5a)
   B. Security in the City (128:5b)
   C. Security for the Country (128:6)

⬥ PSALM 129 ⬥

ISRAEL AND HER FOES

I. ISRAEL VICTIMIZED (129:1–3)
   A. Frequent Persecution (129:1)
   B. Fruitless Persecution (129:2)
   C. Frightful Persecution (129:3)
II. ISRAEL VINDICATED (129:4–8)
   A. The Lord's Righteousness Declared (129:4)
   B. The Lord's Retribution Desired (129:5–8)
      1. Their Unsuccessful Schemes (129:5)
      2. Their Unproductive Show (129:6–7)
      3. Their Unblessed Souls (129:8)

PSALM 130

A PENITENTIAL PSALM

I. PERSONAL EXPERIENCE (130:1–6)
   A. The Psalmist Is Depressed (130:1–2)
      1. Desperate Condition (130:1)
      2. Desperate Cry (130:2)
   B. The Psalmist Is Defiled (130:3–4)
      1. A Sad Fact (130:3)
      2. A Sure Forgiveness (130:4)
   C. The Psalmist Is Determined (130:5–6)
      1. Spiritual Exercise (130:5)
      2. Splendid Expectation (130:6)
II. PUBLIC EXHORTATION (130:7–8)
   A. There Is Hope in the Lord (130:7)
   B. There Is Help in the Lord (130:8)

⮐PSALM 131⮐

A HUMBLE BELIEVER

I. TRUE HUMILITY (131:1–2)
    A. Crucified Pride (131:1)
    B. Cautious Prudence (131:2)
       Beware of:
       1. Undue Independence
       2. Undue Insecurity
II. TRIUMPHANT HOPE (131:3)

PSALM 132

GOD'S COVENANT WITH DAVID

I. DAVID'S OATH RECORDED BY THE LORD (132:1–10)
   A. A Reminder of David's Sincerity (132:1–7)
      1. David's Afflictions (132:1)
      2. David's Affirmations (132:2–7)
         a. Wording of the Pledge (132:2–5)
            David promised he would be:
            (1) Truthful in His Promise (132:2)
            (2) Tireless in His Purpose (132:3–4)
            (3) Triumphant in His Performance (132:5)
         b. Witnesses to the Pledge (132:6–7)
   B. A Request for David's Sake (132:8–10)
      The matter of:
      1. A Finished Work (132:8)
      2. A Faltering Worship (132:9)
      3. A Fervent Wish (132:10)
II. DAVID'S OATH RECIPROCATED BY THE LORD (132:11–18)
   A. The Promise Regarding the Scepter (132:11–12)
      1. The Lord's Integrity (132:11a)
      2. The Lord's Intention (132:11b–12)
   B. The Promise Regarding the Sanctuary (132:13–15)
      1. A Selected Place (132:13)
      2. A Sacred Place (132:14)
      3. A Satisfying Place (132:15)
   C. The Promise Regarding the Saints (132:16)
   D. The Promise Regarding the Site (132:17–18)
      A central point for:
      1. Vitality (132:17)
      2. Victory (132:18)

⌐PSALM 133⌐

THE UNITY OF THE SPIRIT

I. THE BEAUTY OF UNITY (133:1–3a)
    A. A Declaration About Unity (133:1)
    B. A Description of Unity (133:2–3a)
    C. An Illustration from the Sacred Realm—We are taken to the cloister and shown a ministering priest
    D. An illustration from the Secular Realm—We are taken to the country and shown a mountain pasture
II. THE BLESSING OF UNITY (133:3b)

PSALM 134

WITHOUT A CLOUD BETWEEN

I. RENDERING BLESSING TO THE LORD (134:1–2)
   A. Who (134:1a)
   B. When (134:1b)
   C. Where (134:1c–2)
   D. What (134:2a)
II. RECEIVING BLESSING FROM THE LORD (134:3)
   A. The Lord's Ability (134:3a)
   B. The Lord's Abode (134:3b)

⌐ PSALM 135 ⌐

WORSHIP

I. INVOKED WORSHIP (135:1–2)
Worship should be inspired by:
A. His Person (135:1a)
B. Our Position (135:1b–2)
II. INTELLIGENT WORSHIP (135:3–14)
A. For His Goodness (135:3–4)
   1. His Personal Charm (135:3)
   2. His Peculiar Choice (135:4)
B. For His Greatness (135:5–13)
   1. Declared (135:5)
   2. Displayed (135:6–12)
     a. His Creation Is a Witness (135:6–7)
     b. His Conquests Are a Witness (135:8–12)
   3. Described (135:13)
C. For His Government (135:14)
III. INSENSATE WORSHIP (135:15–18)
A. The Foolishness of Idolatry (135:15–17)
   1. Idols Are Manufactured (135:15)
   2. Idols Are Meaningless (135:16–17)
B. The Foolishness of Idolators (135:18)
IV. INSISTENT WORSHIP (135:19–20)
A. Full Participation in Worship (135:20)
   1. By the People (135:19a)
   2. By the Priests (135:19b–20a)
   3. By the Proselytes (135:20b)
B. Fervent Participation in Worship (135:21)

∽ PSALM 136 ∽

THE KINDNESS OF GOD

I. THE CALL TO THANKSGIVING (136:1–3)
   A. The Goodness of God (136:1)
   B. The Greatness of God (136:2–3)
      1. His Deity (136:2)
      2. His Dominion (136:3)
II. THE CAUSES OF THANKSGIVING (136:4–25)
   A. The Lord Created All Things (136:4–9)
      1. God's Personal Uniqueness (136:4)
      2. God's Perfect Universe (136:5–9)
         a. The Original Chaos (136:5–6)
         b. The Original Cosmos (136:7–9)
   B. The Lord Controls All Things (136:10–24)
      1. How the Lord Delivered Israel (136:10–15)
         a. His First Act of Deliverance (136:10)
         b. His Further Act of Deliverance (136:11–14)
            (1) In Saving Them (136:11–12)
            (2) In Separating Them (136:13–14)
         c. His Final Act of Deliverance (136:15)
      2. How the Lord Directed Israel (136:16–22)
         a. In Their Ways (136:16)
         b. In Their Wars (136:17–22)
            (1) Their Conspicuous Triumphs (136:17–20)
            (2) Their Conquered Territory (136:21–22)
      3. How the Lord Defended Israel (136:23–24)
         a. Remembered Them (136:23)
         b. Rescued Them (136:24)
   C. The Lord Considers All Things (136:25)
III. THE CONCLUSION OF THANKSGIVING (136:26)

☞ PSALM 137 ☜

JERUSALEM, BABYLON, AND EDOM

I. THE WOEFUL MISERY OF THE EXILES (137:1–4)
   A. The Distress of the Captives (137:1–2)
      1. The Waters of Babylon (137:1a)
      2. The Wistfulness of Babylon (137:1b)
      3. The Willows of Babylon (137:2)
   B. The Demand of the Conquerors (137:3–4)
      1. What the Conquerors Required (137:3)
      2. What the Captives Replied (137:4)
II. THE WAKENED MEMORY OF THE EXILES (137:5–9)
   A. How Favored Jerusalem Was (137:5–6)
      The memory of it should color:
      1. Every Pursuit of Life (137:5–6a)
      2. Every Pleasure of Life (137:6b)
   B. How Fitting Judgment Was (137:7–9)
      1. The Vicious Attitude of Edom (137:7)
      2. The Violent Atrocities of Babylon (137:8–9)

PSALM 138

TRUSTING WHEN THINGS GO WRONG

I. GLADNESS (138:1–2)
    A. David's Inner Compulsion to Worship (138:1)
       1. Its Totality (138:1a)
       2. Its Testimony (138:1b)
    B. David's Inspired Comprehension of Worship (138:2)
       1. The Temple That Was So Solidly Real to Him (138:2a)
       2. The Topic That Was So Sweetly Refreshing to Him (138:2b)
       3. The Truth That Was So Suddenly Revealed to Him (138:2c)

II. GRACE (138:3)

III. GLORY (138:4–5)

IV. GOVERNMENT (138:6–7)
    A. An Amazing Fact (138:6)
    B. An Abundant Faith (138:7)
       1. God Will Revive Him (138:7a)
       2. God Will Rescue Him (138:7b)

V. GROWTH (138:8)

⁓ PSALM 139 ⁓

FROM EVERLASTING THOU ART

I. WHAT THE PSALMIST REALIZED (139:1–18)
   A. The Truth of God's Omniscience (139:1–6)
      1. David's Examination of This Truth (139:1–5)
         a. The Truth Stated (139:1)
         b. The Truth Studied (139:2–5)
            (1) You See My Every Movement (139:2a)
            (2) You Sound My Every Motive (139:2b)
            (3) You Search My Every Moment (139:3–4)
               (a) My Walk—Every Single Step (139:3)
               (b) My Talk—Every Single Statement (139:4)
            (4) You Surround My Every Maneuver (139:5)
      2. David's Exclamation at This Truth (139:6)
   B. The Truth of God's Omnipresence (139:7–12)
      1. Death Does Not Hide Us from God (139:7–8)
      2. Distance Does Not Hide Us from God (139:9–10)
      3. Darkness Does Not Hide Us from God (139:11–12)
   C. The Truth of God's Omnipotence (139:13–18)
      1. He Created Me (139:13–16)
      2. He Considers Me (139:17–18)
II. WHAT THE PSALMIST REQUESTED (139:19–24)
   A. That the Lord Would Save Him (139:19–22)
      1. David's Assurance (139:19–20)
      2. David's Assertion (139:21–22)
   B. That the Lord Would Search Him (139:23–24)

～PSALM 140～

DELIVERANCE FROM THE WICKED

I. ASKING FOR DELIVERANCE (140:1–11)
   We note how David:
   A. Places His Case Before the Lord (140:1)
   B. Pleads His Case Before the Lord (140:2–11)
      How the evil man's plans are:
      1. Conceived (140:2–4)
         a. Belligerent Thoughts (140:2)
         b. Bitter Words (140:3)
         c. Brutal Deeds (140:4)
      2. Conducted (140:5)
      3. Confounded (140:6–11)
         By:
         a. A God Who Responds (140:6–7)
         b. A God Who Restrains (140:8)
         c. A God Who Rules (140:9–11)
II. ASSURANCE OF DELIVERANCE (140:12–13)
   A. For Those Rejected by Men (140:12)
   B. For Those Right with God (140:13)

A CUNNING PLOT

I. DAVID'S DEVOTION (141:1–2)
    He was looking for:
    A. Action from His Prayer (141:1)
    B. Acceptance of His Prayer (141:2)
II. DAVID'S DESIRE (141:3–4)
    He wanted God to guard him in:
    A. His Conversation (141:3)
    B. His Conduct (141:4a)
    C. His Companionships (141:4b)
III. DAVID'S DISCERNMENT (141:5–6)
    A. The Faithful Rebuke of the Saints (141:5)
    B. The False Reasoning of the Sinner (141:6)
IV. DAVID'S DISMAY (141:7)
V. DAVID'S DEFENSE (141:8–10)
    A. Lord, My Soul Is Destitute (141:8)
    B. Lord, My Situation Is Desperate (141:9–10)

PSALM 142

DOWN IN THE VALLEY

I. THE DISTRESSED MAN (142:1–2)
   A. His Spoken Request (142:1)
   B. His Specific Request (142:2)
      1. The Complaint on His Lips (142:2a)
      2. The Complication in His Life (142:2b)
II. THE DESPERATE MAN (142:3–4)
   A. He Was Fearful (142:3)
      1. Pressures Within (142:3a)
      2. Problems Without (142:3b)
   B. He Was Friendless (142:4)
      1. Treated with Social Indifference (142:4a)
      2. Treated with Spiritual Indifference (142:4b)
III. THE DISCERNING MAN (142:5–6)
   He found in God:
   A. A Satisfying Portion (142:5)
   B. A Secure Protection (142:6)
IV. THE DELIVERED MAN (142:7)
   He was brought into the prospect of:
   A. Freedom (142:7a)
   B. Fellowship (142:7b)
   C. Fullness (142:7c)

PSALM 143

DEPRESSION

I. DAVID'S APPEAL (143:1–4)
   A. Lord, Answer Me (143:1)
   B. Lord, Aid Me (143:2–4)
      1. My Soul Is Doomed (143:2)
      2. My Safety Is Destroyed (143:3)
      3. My Spirit Is Desolate (143:4)

II. DAVID'S ATTITUDE (143:5–6)
   A. Lord, I Am Awed by Your Power—I Long to Apprehend You More Completely (143:5)
   B. Lord, I Am Aware of Your Presence—I Long to Approach You More Closely (143:6)

III. DAVID'S ASPIRATIONS (143:7–12)
   He wanted the Lord to:
   A. Discern Him (143:7)
   B. Direct Him (143:8–10)
   To know something of:
      1. Your Way (143:8)
      2. Your Welcome (143:9)
      3. Your Will (143:10)
   C. Deliver Him (143:11–12)
      1. Give Him Life (143:11)
      2. Give Him Liberty (143:12)

PSALM 144

A Happy People

I. DAVID'S SOURCE OF VITALITY (144:1–2)
   His fame as:
   A. A Soldier (144:1)
   B. A Sovereign (144:2)
II. DAVID'S SENSE OF VANITY (144:3–8)
   A. The Vanity of Man's Person (144:3–4)
      1. How Insignificant Is Our Existence (144:3)
      2. How Inconsequential Is Our Experience (144:4)
   B. The Vanity of Man's Plans (144:5–8)
      1. Apprehending the Power of God (144:5–6)
      2. Appropriating the Power of God (144:7–8)
III. DAVID'S SONG OF VICTORY (144:9–15)
   A. His Determination (144:9)
   B. His Discernment (144:10–11)
      God delivers kings from those who would:
      1. Destroy Them (144:10)
      2. Defame Them (144:11)
   C. His Desire (144:12–15)
      1. For a Magnificent Population (144:12)
      2. For a Manifest Prosperity (144:13–14a)
      3. For a Meaningful Peace (144:14b–c)
      4. For a Mirthful People (144:15)

PSALM 145

A WONDERFUL GOD

I. GOD'S GREATNESS (145:1–6)
   A. The Thoroughness of David's Praise (145:1–2)
      1. Why He Wanted to Praise God (145:1)
         a. God's Personal Relationship to Him (145:1a)
         b. God's Permanent Rule over Him (145:1b)
      2. When He Wanted to Praise God (145:2)
   B. The Theme of David's Praise (145:3–6)
      1. The Awesome Mystery of God's Person (145:3)
      2. The Awesome Might of God's Power (145:4)
      3. The Awesome Majesty of God's Purpose (145:5)
      4. The Awesome Meaning of God's Providence (145:6)
II. GOD'S GOODNESS (145:7–10)
   A. The Moral Goodness of God (145:7)
   B. The Merciful Goodness of God (145:8)
   C. The Manifold Goodness of God (145:9)
   D. The Meaningful Goodness of God (145:10)
III. GOD'S GLORY (145:11–13)
   A. God's Inspiring Kingdom (145:11–12)
   B. God's Invincible Kingdom (145:13)

IV. GOD'S GOVERNMENT (145:14–17)
   A. Based on True Kindness (145:14)
   B. Based on True Kingliness (145:15–17)
      1. Absolute Impartiality (145:15–16)
      2. Absolute Impeccability (145:17)
V. GOD'S GRACE (145:18–21)
   A. How God's Grace Is Reviewed (145:18–20a)
      1. How Approachable God Is (145:18)
      2. How Appealing God Is (145:19–20a)
   B. How God's Grace Is Revoked (145:20b)

   C. How God's Grace Is Rhapsodized (145:21)

⌒ PSALM 146 ⌒

GOD CARES

I. TRIUMPH (146:1–2)
  A. Praise Deliberately Provoked (146:1)
  B. Praise Distinctly Promised (146:2)
II. TRUST (146:3–7)
  A. Misplaced Trust (146:3–4)
    1. Subtle Enticement (146:3)
    2. Simple Error (146:4)
  B. Meaningful Trust (146:5–7)
    1. Our Song (146:5)
    2. His Strength (146:6–7)
      a. Strength to Create a Universe (146:6)
      b. Strength to Control a Universe (146:7)
III. TRUTH (146:8–10)
  A. God's Infinite Mercy (146:8a)
  B. God's Inflexible Morality (146:8b–9)
  C. God's Invincible Majesty (146:10)

THE GOODNESS OF GOD

I. GOD AND HIS PRAISE (147:1)
    A. The Psalmist's Appeal (147:1a)
    B. The Psalmist's Appreciation (147:1b)
II. GOD AND HIS PITY (147:2–3)
    A. Israel's Broken Home Being Rebuilt (147:2)
    B. Israel's Broken Heart Being Revived (147:3)
III. GOD AND HIS POWER (147:4–6)
    A. The Greatness of God's Comprehension (147:4–5)
       1. Its Exactness (147:4)
       2. Its Extent (147:5)
    B. The Greatness of God's Compassion (147:6)
IV. GOD AND HIS PROVIDENCE (147:7–9)
    A. It Should Make Us Thankful (147:7)
    B. It Should Make Us Thoughtful (147:8–9)
V. GOD AND HIS PLEASURE (147:10–11)
    A. What Disinterests God (147:10)
    B. What Delights God (147:11)
VI. GOD AND HIS PROTECTION (147:12–14)
    A. The Bulwarks of the Almighty (147:12–13a)
    B. The Blessing of the Almighty (147:13b–14)
VII. GOD AND HIS PURPOSES (147:15–18)
    At God's word:
    A. Winter Starts (147:15–17)
    B. Winter Stops (147:18)
VIII. GOD AND HIS PRECEPTS (147:19–20)
    The possession of them was:
    A. Israel's Exalted Privilege (147:19)
    B. Israel's Exclusive Privilege (147:20)

⁓PSALM 148⁓

PRAISE HIM ALL CREATURES
GREAT AND SMALL

I. PRAISE HIM! HIGH IN THE GLORY (148:1–6)
  A. Where God Should Be Praised (148:1–4)
    1. Where the Spirits Reside (148:1–2)
    2. Where the Stars Revolve (148:3)
    3. Where the Sky Reigns (148:4)
  B. Why God Should Be Praised (148:5–6)
    1. He Originated All Things (148:5)
    2. He Ordains All Things (148:6)
II. PRAISE HIM! HERE ON THIS GLOBE (148:7–14)
  A. The Psalmist Views Our Planet (148:7–10)
    1. The Restless Sea (148:7)
    2. The Raging Storm (148:8)
    3. The Rocky Steeps (148:9a)
    4. The Rural Scene (148:9b–10)
      a. Earth's Flora (148:9b)
      b. Earth's Fauna (148:10)
  B. The Psalmist Views All Peoples (148:11–14)
    1. The Heathen (148:11–13)
      a. The Call to Praise (148:11–12)
      b. The Cause for Praise (148:13)
    2. The Hebrews (148:14)
      a. The Power They Enjoy (148:14a)
      b. The Privilege They Enjoy (148:14b)
      c. The Position They Enjoy (148:14c)

⌒ PSALM 149 ⌒

THE SONG OF THE SWORD

I. THE SONG (149:1–3)
   A. The Theme (149:1a)
   B. The Throng (149:1b–3)
      1. The Great Congregation of Israel Is Assembled (149:1b)
      2. The Great Creator of Israel Is Acclaimed (149:2–3)
         a. O! What a King! (149:2)
         b. O! How We Sing! (149:3)
II. THE SAINTS (149:4–5)
   A. Their Blessing (149:4a)
   B. Their Beauty (149:4b)
   C. Their Bliss (149:5)
III. THE SWORD (149:6–9)
   A. Trusting in That Sword (149:6)
      1. What Must First Be in Our Heart (149:6a)
      2. What May Then Be in Our Hand (149:6b)
   B. Thrusting with That Sword (149:7–9)
      1. In Vengeance (149:7–8)
      2. As Viceroys (149:9)

———•———

PSALM 150

THE HALLELUJAH CHORUS

I. THE PROPER AUDITORIUM (150:1)
   A. The Sacred Auditorium Below (150:1a)
   B. The Spacious Auditorium Above (150:1b)
II. THE PEALING ANTHEM (150:2)
III. THE PERFECT ACCOMPANIMENT (150:3–5)
   A. The Trumpet Call (150:3a)
   B. The Triumphant Chords (150:3b-4)
   C. The Tremendous Crescendo (150:5)
IV. THE PARTICIPATING AUDIENCE (150:6)